On Making
Smart Decisions

HBR's 10 Must Reads series is the definitive collection of ideas and best practices for aspiring and experienced leaders alike. These books offer essential reading selected from the pages of *Harvard Business Review* on topics critical to the success of every manager.

Titles include:

HBR's 10 Must Reads on Change Management
HBR's 10 Must Reads on Collaboration
HBR's 10 Must Reads on Communication
HBR's 10 Must Reads on Innovation
HBR's 10 Must Reads on Leadership
HBR's 10 Must Reads on Making Smart Decisions
HBR's 10 Must Reads on Managing People
HBR's 10 Must Reads on Managing Yourself
HBR's 10 Must Reads on Strategic Marketing
HBR's 10 Must Reads on Strategy
HBR's 10 Must Reads on Teams
HBR's 10 Must Reads: The Essentials

On
Making
Smart
Decisions

HARVARD BUSINESS REVIEW PRESS
Boston, Massachusetts

The web addresses referenced in this book were live and correct at the time of
book's publication but may be subject to change.

Library of Congress Cataloging-in-Publication Data

HBR's 10 must reads on making smart decisions.
     pages cm.—(HBR's 10 must reads series)
  ISBN 978-1-4221-8989-4 (alk. paper)
  1. Decision making.   I. Harvard business review.   II. Title: HBR's ten must
reads on making smart decisions.
  HD30.23.H39 2013
  658.4'03—dc23

                                                        2012045971

The paper used in this publication meets the requirements of the American
National Standard for Permanence of Paper for Publications and Documents in
Libraries and Archives Z39.48-1992.

Contents

HBR'S
10
MUST
READS

On Making
Smart Decisions

The Hidden Traps in Decision Making

by John S. Hammond, Ralph L. Keeney, and Howard Raiffa

MAKING DECISIONS IS THE MOST important job of any executive. It's also the toughest and the riskiest. Bad decisions can damage a business and a career, sometimes irreparably. So where do bad decisions come from? In many cases, they can be traced back to the way the decisions were made—the alternatives were not clearly defined, the right information was not collected, the costs and benefits were not accurately weighed. But sometimes the fault lies not in the decision-making process but rather in the mind of the decision maker. The way the human brain works can sabotage our decisions.

Researchers have been studying the way our minds function in making decisions for half a century. This research, in the laboratory and in the field, has revealed that we use unconscious routines to cope with the complexity inherent in most decisions. These routines, known as *heuristics,* serve us well in most situations. In judging distance, for example, our minds frequently rely on a heuristic that equates clarity with proximity. The clearer an object appears, the closer we judge it to be. The fuzzier it appears, the farther away we assume it must be. This simple mental shortcut helps us to make the continuous stream of distance judgments required to navigate the world.

Yet, like most heuristics, it is not foolproof. On days that are hazier than normal, our eyes will tend to trick our minds into thinking that things are more distant than they actually are. Because the resulting distortion poses few dangers for most of us, we can safely ignore it. For airline pilots, though, the distortion can be catastrophic. That's why pilots are trained to use objective measures of distance in addition to their vision.

Researchers have identified a whole series of such flaws in the way we think in making decisions. Some, like the heuristic for clarity, are sensory misperceptions. Others take the form of biases. Others appear simply as irrational anomalies in our thinking. What makes all these traps so dangerous is their invisibility. Because they are hardwired into our thinking process, we fail to recognize them—even as we fall right into them.

For executives, whose success hinges on the many day-to-day decisions they make or approve, the psychological traps are especially dangerous. They can undermine everything from new-product development to acquisition and divestiture strategy to succession planning. While no one can rid his or her mind of these ingrained flaws, anyone can follow the lead of airline pilots and learn to understand the traps and compensate for them.

In this article, we examine a number of well-documented psychological traps that are particularly likely to undermine business decisions. In addition to reviewing the causes and manifestations of these traps, we offer some specific ways managers can guard against them. It's important to remember, though, that the best defense is always awareness. Executives who attempt to familiarize themselves with these traps and the diverse forms they take will be better able to ensure that the decisions they make are sound and that the recommendations proposed by subordinates or associates are reliable.

The Anchoring Trap

How would you answer these two questions?

- Is the population of Turkey greater than 35 million?

- What's your best estimate of Turkey's population?

Idea in Brief

Bad decisions can often be traced back to the way the decisions were made—the alternatives were not clearly defined, the right information was not collected, the costs and benefits were not accurately weighed. But sometimes the fault lies not in the decision-making process but rather in the mind of the decision maker: The way the human brain works can sabotage the choices we make. In this article, first published in 1998, John S. Hammond, Ralph L. Keeney, and Howard Raiffa examine eight psychological traps that can affect the way we make business decisions. The anchoring trap leads us to give disproportionate weight to the first information we receive. The status-quo trap biases us toward maintaining the current situation—even when better alternatives exist. The sunk-cost trap inclines us to perpetuate the

mistakes of the past. The confirming-evidence trap leads us to seek out information supporting an existing predilection and to discount opposing information. The framing trap occurs when we misstate a problem, undermining the entire decision-making process. The overconfidence trap makes us overestimate the accuracy of our forecasts. The prudence trap leads us to be overcautious when we make estimates about uncertain events. And the recallability trap prompts us to give undue weight to recent, dramatic events. The best way to avoid all the traps is awareness: forewarned is forearmed. But executives can also take other simple steps to protect themselves and their organizations from these mental lapses to ensure that their important business decisions are sound and reliable.

If you're like most people, the figure of 35 million cited in the first question (a figure we chose arbitrarily) influenced your answer to the second question. Over the years, we've posed those questions to many groups of people. In half the cases, we used 35 million in the first question; in the other half, we used 100 million. Without fail, the answers to the second question increase by many millions when the larger figure is used in the first question. This simple test illustrates the common and often pernicious mental phenomenon known as *anchoring*. When considering a decision, the mind gives disproportionate weight to the first information it receives. Initial impressions, estimates, or data anchor subsequent thoughts and judgments.

Anchors take many guises. They can be as simple and seemingly innocuous as a comment offered by a colleague or a statistic appearing in the morning newspaper. They can be as insidious as a stereotype about a person's skin color, accent, or dress. In business, one of the most common types of anchors is a past event or trend. A marketer attempting to project the sales of a product for the coming year often begins by looking at the sales volumes for past years. The old numbers become anchors, which the forecaster then adjusts based on other factors. This approach, while it may lead to a reasonably accurate estimate, tends to give too much weight to past events and not enough weight to other factors. In situations characterized by rapid changes in the marketplace, historical anchors can lead to poor forecasts and, in turn, misguided choices.

Because anchors can establish the terms on which a decision will be made, they are often used as a bargaining tactic by savvy negotiators. Consider the experience of a large consulting firm that was searching for new office space in San Francisco. Working with a commercial real-estate broker, the firm's partners identified a building that met all their criteria, and they set up a meeting with the building's owners. The owners opened the meeting by laying out the terms of a proposed contract: a ten-year lease; an initial monthly price of $2.50 per square foot; annual price increases at the prevailing inflation rate; all interior improvements to be the tenant's responsibility; an option for the tenant to extend the lease for ten additional years under the same terms. Although the price was at the high end of current market rates, the consultants made a relatively modest counteroffer. They proposed an initial price in the midrange of market rates and asked the owners to share in the renovation expenses, but they accepted all the other terms. The consultants could have been much more aggressive and creative in their counterproposal—reducing the initial price to the low end of market rates, adjusting rates biennially rather than annually, putting a cap on the increases, defining different terms for extending the lease, and so forth—but their thinking was guided by the owners' initial proposal. The consultants had fallen into the anchoring trap, and as a result, they ended up paying a lot more for the space than they had to.

What can you do about it?

The effect of anchors in decision making has been documented in thousands of experiments. Anchors influence the decisions not only of managers, but also of accountants and engineers, bankers and lawyers, consultants and stock analysts. No one can avoid their influence; they're just too widespread. But managers who are aware of the dangers of anchors can reduce their impact by using the following techniques:

- Always view a problem from different perspectives. Try using alternative starting points and approaches rather than sticking with the first line of thought that occurs to you.

- Think about the problem on your own before consulting others to avoid becoming anchored by their ideas.

- Be open-minded. Seek information and opinions from a variety of people to widen your frame of reference and to push your mind in fresh directions.

- Be careful to avoid anchoring your advisers, consultants, and others from whom you solicit information and counsel. Tell them as little as possible about your own ideas, estimates, and tentative decisions. If you reveal too much, your own preconceptions may simply come back to you.

- Be particularly wary of anchors in negotiations. Think through your position before any negotiation begins in order to avoid being anchored by the other party's initial proposal. At the same time, look for opportunities to use anchors to your own advantage—if you're the seller, for example, suggest a high, but defensible, price as an opening gambit.

The Status-Quo Trap

We all like to believe that we make decisions rationally and objectively. But the fact is, we all carry biases, and those biases influence the choices we make. Decision makers display, for example, a strong bias toward alternatives that perpetuate the status quo. On a broad scale, we can see this tendency whenever a radically new product is introduced. The first automobiles, revealingly called "horseless carriages," looked very much like the buggies they replaced. The first "electronic newspapers" appearing on the World Wide Web looked very much like their print precursors.

On a more familiar level, you may have succumbed to this bias in your personal financial decisions. People sometimes, for example, inherit shares of stock that they would never have bought themselves. Although it would be a straightforward, inexpensive proposition to sell those shares and put the money into a different investment, a surprising number of people don't sell. They find the status quo comfortable, and they avoid taking action that would upset it. "Maybe I'll rethink it later," they say. But "later" is usually never.

The source of the status-quo trap lies deep within our psyches, in our desire to protect our egos from damage. Breaking from the status quo means taking action, and when we take action, we take responsibility, thus opening ourselves to criticism and to regret. Not surprisingly, we naturally look for reasons to do nothing. Sticking with the status quo represents, in most cases, the safer course because it puts us at less psychological risk.

Many experiments have shown the magnetic attraction of the status quo. In one, a group of people were randomly given one of two gifts of approximately the same value—half received a mug, the other half a Swiss chocolate bar. They were then told that they could easily exchange the gift they received for the other gift. While you might expect that about half would have wanted to make the exchange, only one in ten actually did. The status quo exerted its power even though it had been arbitrarily established only minutes before.

Other experiments have shown that the more choices you are given, the more pull the status quo has. More people will, for instance, choose the status quo when there are two alternatives to it rather than one: A and B instead of just A. Why? Choosing between A and B requires additional effort; selecting the status quo avoids that effort.

In business, where sins of commission (doing something) tend to be punished much more severely than sins of omission (doing nothing), the status quo holds a particularly strong attraction. Many mergers, for example, founder because the acquiring company avoids taking swift action to impose a new, more appropriate management structure on the acquired company. "Let's not rock the boat right now," the typical reasoning goes. "Let's wait until the situation stabilizes." But as time passes, the existing structure becomes more entrenched, and altering it becomes harder, not easier. Having failed to seize the occasion when change would have been expected, management finds itself stuck with the status quo.

What can you do about it?
First of all, remember that in any given decision, maintaining the status quo may indeed be the best choice, but you don't want to choose it just because it is comfortable. Once you become aware of the status-quo trap, you can use these techniques to lessen its pull:

- Always remind yourself of your objectives and examine how they would be served by the status quo. You may find that elements of the current situation act as barriers to your goals.

- Never think of the status quo as your only alternative. Identify other options and use them as counterbalances, carefully evaluating all the pluses and minuses.

- Ask yourself whether you would choose the status-quo alternative if, in fact, it weren't the status quo.

- Avoid exaggerating the effort or cost involved in switching from the status quo.

- Remember that the desirability of the status quo will change over time. When comparing alternatives, always evaluate them in terms of the future as well as the present.

- If you have several alternatives that are superior to the status quo, don't default to the status quo just because you're having a hard time picking the best alternative. Force yourself to choose.

The Sunk-Cost Trap

Another of our deep-seated biases is to make choices in a way that justifies past choices, even when the past choices no longer seem valid. Most of us have fallen into this trap. We may have refused, for example, to sell a stock or a mutual fund at a loss, forgoing other, more attractive investments. Or we may have poured enormous effort into improving the performance of an employee whom we knew we shouldn't have hired in the first place. Our past decisions become what economists term *sunk costs*—old investments of time or money that are now irrecoverable. We know, rationally, that sunk costs are irrelevant to the present decision, but nevertheless they prey on our minds, leading us to make inappropriate decisions.

Why can't people free themselves from past decisions? Frequently, it's because they are unwilling, consciously or not, to admit to a mistake. Acknowledging a poor decision in one's personal life may be purely a private matter, involving only one's self-esteem, but in business, a bad decision is often a very public matter, inviting critical comments from colleagues or bosses. If you fire a poor performer whom you hired, you're making a public admission of poor judgment. It seems psychologically safer to let him or her stay on, even though that choice only compounds the error.

The sunk-cost bias shows up with disturbing regularity in banking, where it can have particularly dire consequences. When a borrower's business runs into trouble, a lender will often advance additional funds in hopes of providing the business with some breathing room to recover. If the business does have a good chance of coming back, that's a wise investment. Otherwise, it's just throwing good money after bad.

One of us helped a major U.S. bank recover after it made many bad loans to foreign businesses. We found that the bankers responsible for originating the problem loans were far more likely to advance additional funds—repeatedly, in many cases—than were bankers who took over the accounts after the original loans were made. Too often, the original bankers' strategy—and loans—ended in failure.

Having been trapped by an escalation of commitment, they had tried, consciously or unconsciously, to protect their earlier, flawed decisions. They had fallen victim to the sunk-cost bias. The bank finally solved the problem by instituting a policy requiring that a loan be immediately reassigned to another banker as soon as any problem arose. The new banker was able to take a fresh, unbiased look at the merit of offering more funds.

Sometimes a corporate culture reinforces the sunk-cost trap. If the penalties for making a decision that leads to an unfavorable outcome are overly severe, managers will be motivated to let failed projects drag on endlessly—in the vain hope that they'll somehow be able to transform them into successes. Executives should recognize that, in an uncertain world where unforeseeable events are common, good decisions can sometimes lead to bad outcomes. By acknowledging that some good ideas will end in failure, executives will encourage people to cut their losses rather than let them mount.

What can you do about it?

For all decisions with a history, you will need to make a conscious effort to set aside any sunk costs—whether psychological or economic—that will muddy your thinking about the choice at hand. Try these techniques:

- Seek out and listen carefully to the views of people who were uninvolved with the earlier decisions and who are hence unlikely to be committed to them.

- Examine why admitting to an earlier mistake distresses you. If the problem lies in your own wounded self-esteem, deal with it head-on. Remind yourself that even smart choices can have bad consequences, through no fault of the original decision maker, and that even the best and most experienced managers are not immune to errors in judgment. Remember the wise words of Warren Buffett: "When you find yourself in a hole, the best thing you can do is stop digging."

- Be on the lookout for the influence of sunk-cost biases in the decisions and recommendations made by your subordinates. Reassign responsibilities when necessary.

- Don't cultivate a failure-fearing culture that leads employees to perpetuate their mistakes. In rewarding people, look at the quality of their decision making (taking into account what was known at the time their decisions were made), not just the quality of the outcomes.

The Confirming-Evidence Trap

Imagine that you're the president of a successful midsize U.S. manufacturer considering whether to call off a planned plant expansion. For a while you've been concerned that your company won't be able to sustain the rapid pace of growth of its exports. You fear that the value of the U.S. dollar will strengthen in coming months, making your goods more costly for overseas consumers and dampening demand. But before you put the brakes on the plant expansion, you decide to call up an acquaintance, the chief executive of a similar company that recently mothballed a new factory, to check her reasoning. She presents a strong case that other currencies are about to weaken significantly against the dollar. What do you do?

You'd better not let that conversation be the clincher, because you've probably just fallen victim to the confirming-evidence bias. This bias leads us to seek out information that supports our existing instinct or point of view while avoiding information that contradicts it. What, after all, did you expect your acquaintance to give, other than a strong argument in favor of her own decision? The confirming-evidence bias not only affects where we go to collect evidence but also how we interpret the evidence we do receive, leading us to give too much weight to supporting information and too little to conflicting information.

In one psychological study of this phenomenon, two groups—one opposed to and one supporting capital punishment—each read two reports of carefully conducted research on the effectiveness of the death penalty as a deterrent to crime. One report concluded that the death penalty was effective; the other concluded it was not. Despite being exposed to solid scientific information supporting counterarguments, the members of both groups became even more convinced of the validity of their own position after reading both reports. They automatically accepted the supporting information and dismissed the conflicting information.

There are two fundamental psychological forces at work here. The first is our tendency to subconsciously decide what we want to do before we figure out why we want to do it. The second is our inclination to be more engaged by things we like than by things we dislike—a tendency well documented even in babies. Naturally, then, we are drawn to information that supports our subconscious leanings.

What can you do about it?

It's not that you shouldn't make the choice you're subconsciously drawn to. It's just that you want to be sure it's the smart choice. You need to put it to the test. Here's how:

- Always check to see whether you are examining all the evidence with equal rigor. Avoid the tendency to accept confirming evidence without question.

- Get someone you respect to play devil's advocate, to argue against the decision you're contemplating. Better yet, build the counterarguments yourself. What's the strongest reason to do something else? The second strongest reason? The third? Consider the position with an open mind.

- Be honest with yourself about your motives. Are you really gathering information to help you make a smart choice, or are you just looking for evidence confirming what you think you'd like to do?

- In seeking the advice of others, don't ask leading questions that invite confirming evidence. And if you find that an adviser always seems to support your point of view, find a new adviser. Don't surround yourself with yes-men.

The Framing Trap

The first step in making a decision is to frame the question. It's also one of the most dangerous steps. The way a problem is framed can profoundly influence the choices you make. In a case involving automobile insurance, for example, framing made a $200 million difference. To reduce insurance costs, two neighboring states, New Jersey and Pennsylvania, made similar changes in their laws. Each state gave drivers a new option: By accepting a limited right to sue, they could lower their premiums. But the two states framed the choice in very different ways: In New Jersey, you automatically got the limited right to sue unless you specified otherwise; in Pennsylvania, you got the full right to sue unless you specified otherwise. The different frames established different status quos, and, not surprisingly, most consumers defaulted to the status quo. As a result, in New Jersey about 80% of drivers chose the limited right to sue, but in Pennsylvania only 25% chose it. Because of the way it framed the choice, Pennsylvania failed to gain approximately $200 million in expected insurance and litigation savings.

The framing trap can take many forms, and as the insurance example shows, it is often closely related to other psychological traps. A frame can establish the status quo or introduce an anchor. It can highlight sunk costs or lead you toward confirming evidence. Decision researchers have documented two types of frames that distort decision making with particular frequency.

Frames as gains versus losses

In a study patterned after a classic experiment by decision researchers Daniel Kahneman and Amos Tversky, one of us posed the following problem to a group of insurance professionals:

> You are a marine property adjuster charged with minimizing the loss of cargo on three insured barges that sank yesterday off the coast of Alaska. Each barge holds $200,000 worth of cargo, which will be lost if not salvaged within 72 hours. The owner of a

local marine-salvage company gives you two options, both of which will cost the same:

Plan A: This plan will save the cargo of one of the three barges, worth $200,000.

Plan B: This plan has a one-third probability of saving the cargo on all three barges, worth $600,000, but has a two-thirds probability of saving nothing.

Which plan would you choose?

If you are like 71% of the respondents in the study, you chose the "less risky" Plan A, which will save one barge for sure. Another group in the study, however, was asked to choose between alternatives C and D:

Plan C: This plan will result in the loss of two of the three cargoes, worth $400,000.

Plan D: This plan has a two-thirds probability of resulting in the loss of all three cargoes and the entire $600,000 but has a one-third probability of losing no cargo.

Faced with this choice, 80% of these respondents preferred Plan D. The pairs of alternatives are, of course, precisely equivalent—Plan A is the same as Plan C, and Plan B is the same as Plan D—they've just been framed in different ways. The strikingly different responses reveal that people are risk averse when a problem is posed in terms of gains (barges saved) but risk seeking when a problem is posed in terms of avoiding losses (barges lost). Furthermore, they tend to adopt the frame as it is presented to them rather than restating the problem in their own way.

Framing with different reference points

The same problem can also elicit very different responses when frames use different reference points. Let's say you have $2,000 in your checking account and you are asked the following question:

Would you accept a fifty-fifty chance of either losing $300 or winning $500?

Would you accept the chance? What if you were asked this question:

Would you prefer to keep your checking account balance of $2,000 or to accept a fifty-fifty chance of having either $1,700 or $2,500 in your account?

Once again, the two questions pose the same problem. While your answers to both questions should, rationally speaking, be the same, studies have shown that many people would refuse the fifty-fifty chance in the first question but accept it in the second. Their different reactions result from the different reference points presented in the two frames. The first frame, with its reference point of zero, emphasizes incremental gains and losses, and the thought of losing triggers a conservative response in many people's minds. The second frame, with its reference point of $2,000, puts things into perspective by emphasizing the real financial impact of the decision.

What can you do about it?

A poorly framed problem can undermine even the best-considered decision. But any adverse effect of framing can be limited by taking the following precautions:

- Don't automatically accept the initial frame, whether it was formulated by you or by someone else. Always try to reframe the problem in various ways. Look for distortions caused by the frames.

- Try posing problems in a neutral, redundant way that combines gains and losses or embraces different reference points. For example: Would you accept a fifty-fifty chance of either losing $300, resulting in a bank balance of $1,700, or winning $500, resulting in a bank balance of $2,500?

- Think hard throughout your decision-making process about the framing of the problem. At points throughout the process, particularly near the end, ask yourself how your thinking might change if the framing changed.

- When others recommend decisions, examine the way they framed the problem. Challenge them with different frames.

The Estimating and Forecasting Traps

Most of us are adept at making estimates about time, distance, weight, and volume. That's because we're constantly making judgments about these variables and getting quick feedback about the accuracy of those judgments. Through daily practice, our minds become finely calibrated.

Making estimates or forecasts about uncertain events, however, is a different matter. While managers continually make such estimates and forecasts, they rarely get clear feedback about their accuracy. If you judge, for example, that the likelihood of the price of oil falling to less than $15 a barrel one year hence is about 40% and the price does indeed fall to that level, you can't tell whether you were right or wrong about the probability you estimated. The only way to gauge your accuracy would be to keep track of many, many similar judgments to see if, after the fact, the events you thought had a 40% chance of occurring actually did occur 40% of the time. That would require a great deal of data, carefully tracked over a long period of time. Weather forecasters and bookmakers have the opportunities and incentives to maintain such records, but the rest of us don't. As a result, our minds never become calibrated for making estimates in the face of uncertainty.

All of the traps we've discussed so far can influence the way we make decisions when confronted with uncertainty. But there's another set of traps that can have a particularly distorting effect in uncertain situations because they cloud our ability to assess probabilities. Let's look at three of the most common of these uncertainty traps.

The overconfidence trap

Even though most of us are not very good at making estimates or forecasts, we actually tend to be overconfident about our accuracy. That can lead to errors in judgment and, in turn, bad decisions.

In one series of tests, people were asked to forecast the next week's closing value for the Dow Jones Industrial Average. To account for uncertainty, they were then asked to estimate a range within which the closing value would likely fall. In picking the top number of the range, they were asked to choose a high estimate they thought had only a 1% chance of being exceeded by the closing value. Similarly, for the bottom end, they were told to pick a low estimate for which they thought there would be only a 1% chance of the closing value falling below it. If they were good at judging their forecasting accuracy, you'd expect the participants to be wrong only about 2% of the time. But hundreds of tests have shown that the actual Dow Jones averages fell outside the forecast ranges 20% to 30% of the time. Overly confident about the accuracy of their predictions, most people set too narrow a range of possibilities.

Think of the implications for business decisions, in which major initiatives and investments often hinge on ranges of estimates. If managers underestimate the high end or overestimate the low end of a crucial variable, they may miss attractive opportunities or expose themselves to far greater risk than they realize. Much money has been wasted on ill-fated product-development projects because managers did not accurately account for the possibility of market failure.

The prudence trap

Another trap for forecasters takes the form of overcautiousness, or prudence. When faced with high-stakes decisions, we tend to adjust our estimates or forecasts "just to be on the safe side." Many years ago, for example, one of the Big Three U.S. automakers was deciding how many of a new-model car to produce in anticipation of its busiest sales season. The market-planning department, responsible for the decision, asked other departments to supply forecasts of key variables such as anticipated sales, dealer inventories, competitor actions, and costs. Knowing the purpose of the estimates, each department slanted its forecast to favor building more cars—"just to be safe." But the market planners took the numbers at face value and then made their own "just to be safe" adjustments. Not surprisingly, the number of cars produced far exceeded demand, and the company took six months to sell off the surplus, resorting in the end to promotional pricing.

Policy makers have gone so far as to codify overcautiousness in formal decision procedures. An extreme example is the methodology of "worst-case analysis," which was once popular in the design of weapons systems and is still used in certain engineering and regulatory settings. Using this approach, engineers designed weapons to operate under the worst possible combination of circumstances, even though the odds of those circumstances actually coming to pass were infinitesimal. Worst-case analysis added enormous costs with no practical benefit (in fact, it often backfired by touching off an arms race), proving that too much prudence can sometimes be as dangerous as too little.

The recallability trap

Even if we are neither overly confident nor unduly prudent, we can still fall into a trap when making estimates or forecasts. Because we frequently base our predictions about future events on our memory of past events, we can be overly influenced by dramatic events—those that leave a strong impression on our memory. We all, for example, exaggerate the probability of rare but catastrophic occurrences such as plane crashes because they get disproportionate attention in the media. A dramatic or traumatic event in your own life can also distort your thinking. You will assign a higher probability to traffic accidents if you have passed one on the way to work, and you will assign a higher chance of someday dying of cancer yourself if a close friend has died of the disease.

In fact, anything that distorts your ability to recall events in a balanced way will distort your probability assessments. In one experiment, lists of well-known men and women were read to different groups of people. Unbeknownst to the subjects, each list had an equal number of men and women, but on some lists the men were more famous than the women while on others the women were more famous. Afterward, the participants were asked to estimate the percentages of men and women on each list. Those who had heard the list with the more famous men thought there were more men on the list, while those who had heard the one with the more famous women thought there were more women.

Corporate lawyers often get caught in the recallability trap when defending liability suits. Their decisions about whether to settle a claim or take it to court usually hinge on their assessments of the possible outcomes of a trial. Because the media tend to aggressively publicize massive damage awards (while ignoring other, far more common trial outcomes), lawyers can overestimate the probability of a large award for the plaintiff. As a result, they offer larger settlements than are actually warranted.

What can you do about it?

The best way to avoid the estimating and forecasting traps is to take a very disciplined approach to making forecasts and judging probabilities. For each of the three traps, some additional precautions can be taken:

- To reduce the effects of overconfidence in making estimates, always start by considering the extremes, the low and high ends of the possible range of values. This will help you avoid being anchored by an initial estimate. Then challenge your estimates of the extremes. Try to imagine circumstances where the actual figure would fall below your low or above your high, and adjust your range accordingly. Challenge the estimates of your subordinates and advisers in a similar fashion. They're also susceptible to overconfidence.

- To avoid the prudence trap, always state your estimates honestly and explain to anyone who will be using them that they have not been adjusted. Emphasize the need for honest input to anyone who will be supplying you with estimates. Test estimates over a reasonable range to assess their impact. Take a second look at the more sensitive estimates.

- To minimize the distortion caused by variations in recallability, carefully examine all your assumptions to ensure they're not unduly influenced by your memory. Get actual statistics whenever possible. Try not to be guided by impressions.

Forewarned Is Forearmed

When it comes to business decisions, there's rarely such a thing as a no-brainer. Our brains are always at work, sometimes, unfortunately, in ways that hinder rather than help us. At every stage of the decision-making process, misperceptions, biases, and other tricks of the mind can influence the choices we make. Highly complex and important decisions are the most prone to distortion because they tend to involve the most assumptions, the most estimates, and the most inputs from the most people. The higher the stakes, the higher the risk of being caught in a psychological trap.

The traps we've reviewed can all work in isolation. But, even more dangerous, they can work in concert, amplifying one another. A dramatic first impression might anchor our thinking, and then we might selectively seek out confirming evidence to justify our initial inclination. We make a hasty decision, and that decision establishes a new status quo. As our sunk costs mount, we become trapped, unable to find a propitious time to seek out a new and possibly better course. The psychological miscues cascade, making it harder and harder to choose wisely.

As we said at the outset, the best protection against all psychological traps—in isolation or in combination—is awareness. Forewarned is forearmed. Even if you can't eradicate the distortions ingrained into the way your mind works, you can build tests and disciplines into your decision-making process that can uncover errors in thinking before they become errors in judgment. And taking action to understand and avoid psychological traps can have the added benefit of increasing your confidence in the choices you make.

Originally published in January 2006. Reprint R0601K

Before You Make
That Big Decision . . .

*by Daniel Kahneman, Dan Lovallo,
and Olivier Sibony*

THANKS TO A SLEW of popular new books, many executives today realize how biases can distort reasoning in business. *Confirmation bias,* for instance, leads people to ignore evidence that contradicts their preconceived notions. *Anchoring* causes them to weigh one piece of information too heavily in making decisions; *loss aversion* makes them too cautious. In our experience, however, awareness of the effects of biases has done little to improve the quality of business decisions at either the individual or the organizational level.

Though there may now be far more talk of biases among managers, talk alone will not eliminate them. But it is possible to take steps to counteract them. A recent McKinsey study of more than 1,000 major business investments showed that when organizations worked at reducing the effect of bias in their decision-making processes, they achieved returns up to seven percentage points higher. (For more on this study, see "The Case for Behavioral Strategy," *McKinsey Quarterly,* March 2010.) Reducing bias makes a difference. In this article, we will describe a straightforward way to detect bias and minimize its effects in the most common kind of decision that executives make: reviewing a recommendation from someone else and determining whether to accept it, reject it, or pass it on to the next level.

For most executives, these reviews seem simple enough. First, they need to quickly grasp the relevant facts (getting them from people who know more about the details than they do). Second, they need to figure out if the people making the recommendation are intentionally clouding the facts in some way. And finally, they need to apply their own experience, knowledge, and reasoning to decide whether the recommendation is right.

However, this process is fraught at every stage with the potential for distortions in judgment that result from cognitive biases. Executives can't do much about their own biases, as we shall see. But given the proper tools, they can recognize and neutralize those of their teams. Over time, by using these tools, they will build decision processes that reduce the effect of biases in their organizations. And in doing so, they'll help upgrade the quality of decisions their organizations make.

The Challenge of Avoiding Bias

Let's delve first into the question of why people are incapable of recognizing their own biases.

According to cognitive scientists, there are two modes of thinking, intuitive and reflective. (In recent decades a lot of psychological research has focused on distinctions between them. Richard Thaler and Cass Sunstein popularized it in their book, *Nudge*.) In intuitive, or System One, thinking, impressions, associations, feelings, intentions, and preparations for action flow effortlessly. System One produces a constant representation of the world around us and allows us to do things like walk, avoid obstacles, and contemplate something else all at the same time. We're usually in this mode when we brush our teeth, banter with friends, or play tennis. We're not consciously focusing on how to do those things; we just do them.

In contrast reflective, or System Two, thinking is slow, effortful, and deliberate. This mode is at work when we complete a tax form or learn to drive. Both modes are continuously active, but System Two is typically just monitoring things. It's mobilized when the stakes are

Idea in Brief

When an executive makes a big bet, he or she typically relies on the judgment of a team that has put together a proposal for a strategic course of action. After all, the team will have delved into the pros and cons much more deeply than the executive has time to do. The problem is, biases invariably creep into any team's reasoning—and often dangerously distort its thinking. A team that has fallen in love with its recommendation, for instance, may subconsciously dismiss evidence that contradicts its theories, give far too much weight to one piece of data, or make faulty comparisons to another business case. That's why, with important decisions, executives need to conduct a careful review not only of the content of recommendations but of the recommendation process. To that end, the authors— Kahneman, who won a Nobel Prize in economics for his work on cognitive biases; Lovallo of the University of Sydney; and Sibony of McKinsey—have put together a 12-question checklist intended to unearth and neutralize defects in teams' thinking. These questions help leaders examine whether a team has explored alternatives appropriately, gathered all the right information, and used well-grounded numbers to support its case. They also highlight considerations such as whether the team might be unduly influenced by self-interest, overconfidence, or attachment to past decisions. By using this practical tool, executives will build decision processes over time that reduce the effects of biases and upgrade the quality of decisions their organizations make. The payoffs can be significant: A recent McKinsey study of more than 1,000 business investments, for instance, showed that when companies worked to reduce the effects of bias, they raised their returns on investment by seven percentage points. Executives need to realize that the judgment of even highly experienced, superbly competent managers can be fallible. A disciplined decision-making process, not individual genius, is the key to good strategy.

high, when we detect an obvious error, or when rule-based reasoning is required. But most of the time, System One determines our thoughts.

Our visual system and associative memory (both important aspects of System One) are designed to produce a single coherent interpretation of what is going on around us. That sense making is highly sensitive to context. Consider the word "bank." For most

The Behavioral Economics
of Decision Making

DANIEL KAHNEMAN (THE LEAD AUTHOR) and Amos Tversky introduced the idea of cognitive biases, and their impact on decision making, in 1974. Their research and ideas were recognized when Kahneman was awarded a Nobel Prize in economics in 2002. These biases, and behavioral psychology generally, have since captured the imagination of business experts. Below are some notable popular books on this topic:

> *Nudge: Improving Decisions About Health, Wealth, and Happiness* by Richard H. Thaler and Cass R. Sunstein (Caravan, 2008)

> *Think Twice: Harnessing the Power of Counterintuition* by Michael J. Mauboussin (Harvard Business Review Press, 2009)

> *Think Again: Why Good Leaders Make Bad Decisions and How to Keep It from Happening to You* by Sydney Finkelstein, Jo Whitehead, and Andrew Campbell (Harvard Business Review Press, 2009)

> *Predictably Irrational: The Hidden Forces That Shape Our Decisions* by Dan Ariely (HarperCollins, 2008)

> *Thinking, Fast and Slow* by Daniel Kahneman (Farrar, Straus and Giroux, 2011)

people reading HBR, it would signify a financial institution. But if the same readers encountered this word in *Field & Stream,* they would probably understand it differently. Context is complicated: In addition to visual cues, memories, and associations, it comprises goals, anxieties, and other inputs. As System One makes sense of those inputs and develops a narrative, it suppresses alternative stories.

Because System One is so good at making up contextual stories and we're not aware of its operations, it can lead us astray. The stories it creates are generally accurate, but there are exceptions. Cognitive biases are one major, well-documented example. An insidious feature of cognitive failures is that we have no way of knowing that they're happening: We almost never catch ourselves in the act of making intuitive errors. Experience doesn't help us recognize them. (By contrast, if we tackle a difficult problem using System Two thinking and fail to solve it, we're uncomfortably aware of that fact.)

Preliminary Questions

Ask yourself

1. **Check for self-interested biases**

   Is there any reason to suspect the team making the recommendation of errors motivated by self-interest?

   Review the proposal with extra care, especially for overoptimism.

2. **Check for the affect heuristic**

   Has the team fallen in love with its proposal?

   Rigorously apply all the quality controls on the checklist.

3. **Check for groupthink**

   Were there dissenting opinions within the team?

   Were they explored adequately?

   Solicit dissenting views, discreetly if necessary.

This inability to sense that we've made a mistake is the key to understanding why we generally accept our intuitive, effortless thinking at face value. It also explains why, even when we become aware of the existence of biases, we're not excited about eliminating them in ourselves. After all, it's difficult for us to fix errors we can't see.

By extension, this also explains why the management experts writing about cognitive biases have not provided much practical help. Their overarching theme is "forewarned is forearmed." But knowing you have biases is not enough to help you overcome them. You may accept that you have biases, but you cannot eliminate them in yourself.

There is reason for hope, however, when we move from the individual to the collective, from the decision maker to the decision-making process, and from the executive to the organization. As researchers have documented in the realm of operational management, the fact that individuals are not aware of their own biases does not mean that biases can't be neutralized—or at least reduced—at the organizational level.

Challenge Questions

Ask the recommenders

4. **Check for saliency bias**

   Could the diagnosis be overly influenced by an analogy to a memorable success?

   Ask for more analogies, and rigorously analyze their similarity to the current situation.

5. **Check for confirmation bias**

   Are credible alternatives included along with the recommendation?

   Request additional options.

6. **Check for availability bias**

   If you had to make this decision again in a year's time, what information would you want, and can you get more of it now?

   Use checklists of the data needed for each kind of decision.

7. **Check for anchoring bias**

   Do you know where the numbers came from? Can there be

   . . . unsubstantiated numbers?

   . . . extrapolation from history?

   . . . a motivation to use a certain anchor?

   Reanchor with figures generated by other models or benchmarks, and request new analysis.

8. **Check for halo effect**

   Is the team assuming that a person, organization, or approach that is successful in one area will be just as successful in another?

   Eliminate false inferences, and ask the team to seek additional comparable examples.

9. **Check for sunk-cost fallacy, endowment effect**

   Are the recommenders overly attached to a history of past decisions?

   Consider the issue as if you were a new CEO.

Evaluation Questions

Ask about the proposal

10. **Check for overconfidence, planning fallacy, optimistic biases, competitor neglect**

    Is the base case overly optimistic?

    Have the team build a case taking an outside view; use war games.

11. **Check for disaster neglect**

    Is the worst case bad enough?

    Have the team conduct a premortem: Imagine that the worst has happened, and develop a story about the causes.

12. **Check for loss aversion**

    Is the recommending team overly cautious?

    Realign incentives to share responsibility for the risk or to remove risk.

This is true because most decisions are influenced by many people, and because decision makers can turn their ability to spot biases in others' thinking to their own advantage. We may not be able to control our own intuition, but we can apply rational thought to detect others' faulty intuition and improve *their* judgment. (In other words, we can use our System Two thinking to spot System One errors in the recommendations given to us by others.)

This is precisely what executives are expected to do every time they review recommendations and make a final call. Often they apply a crude, unsystematic adjustment—such as adding a "safety margin" to a forecasted cost—to account for a perceived bias. For the most part, however, decision makers focus on *content* when they review and challenge recommendations. We propose adding a systematic review of the recommendation *process,* one aimed at identifying the biases that may have influenced the people putting forth proposals. The idea is to retrace their steps to determine where intuitive thinking may have steered them off-track.

In the following section, we'll walk you through how to do a process review, drawing on the actual experiences of three corporate executives—Bob, Lisa, and Devesh (not their real names)—who were asked to consider very different kinds of proposals:

A radical pricing change. Bob is the vice president of sales in a business services company. Recently, his senior regional VP and several colleagues recommended a total overhaul of the company's pricing structure. They argued that the company had lost a number of bids to competitors, as well as some of its best salespeople, because of unsustainable price levels. But making the wrong move could be very costly and perhaps even trigger a price war.

A large capital outlay. Lisa is the chief financial officer of a capital-intensive manufacturing company. The VP of manufacturing in one of the corporation's business units has proposed a substantial investment in one manufacturing site. The request has all the usual components—a revenue forecast, an analysis of return on investment under various scenarios, and so on. But the investment would be a very large one—in a business that has been losing money for some time.

A major acquisition. Devesh is the CEO of a diversified industrial company. His business development team has proposed purchasing a firm whose offerings would complement the product line in one of the company's core businesses. However, the potential deal comes on the heels of several successful but expensive takeovers, and the company's financial structure is stretched.

While we are intentionally describing this review from the perspective of the individual decision makers, organizations can also take steps to embed some of these practices in their broader decision-making processes. (For the best ways to approach that, see the sidebar "Improving Decisions Throughout the Organization.")

Decision Quality Control: A Checklist

To help executives vet decisions, we have developed a tool, based on a 12-question checklist, that is intended to unearth defects in thinking—in other words, the cognitive biases of the teams making recommendations. The questions fall into three categories: questions the decision makers should ask themselves, questions they should use to challenge the people proposing a course of action, and questions aimed at evaluating the proposal. It's important to note that, because you can't recognize your own biases, the individuals using this quality screen should be completely independent from the teams making the recommendations.

Questions that decision makers should ask themselves

1. Is there any reason to suspect *motivated errors*, or errors driven by the self-interest of the recommending team? Decision makers should never directly ask the people making the proposal this. After all, it's nearly impossible to do so without appearing to question their diligence and even their integrity, and that conversation cannot end well.

The issue here is not just intentional deception. People do sometimes lie deliberately, of course, but self-deception and rationalization are more common problems. Research has shown that professionals who sincerely believe that their decisions are "not for sale" (such as physicians) are still biased in the direction of their own interests.

Bob, for instance, should recognize that lowering prices to respond to competitive pressures will have a material impact on the commissions of his sales team (especially if bonuses are based on revenues, not margins). Devesh should wonder whether the team recommending the acquisition would expect to run the acquired company and therefore might be influenced by "empire building" motives.

Of course, a preference for a particular outcome is built into every recommendation. Decision makers need to assess not whether there's a risk of motivated error but whether it is significant. A proposal from a set of individuals who stand to gain more than usual from the outcome—either in financial terms or, more frequently, in terms of organizational power, reputation, or career options—needs especially careful quality control. Reviewers also should watch out for pernicious sets of options that include only one realistic alternative—the one that the recommending team prefers. In such cases, decision makers will have to pay even more attention to the remaining questions on this checklist, particularly those covering optimistic biases.

2. Have the people making the recommendation fallen in love with it? All of us are subject to the *affect heuristic:* When evaluating something we like, we tend to minimize its risks and costs and exaggerate its benefits; when assessing something we dislike, we do the opposite. Executives often observe this phenomenon in decisions with a strong emotional component, such as those concerning employees, brands, or locations.

This question is also best left unspoken but is usually easy to answer. It is likely that Devesh will easily sense whether the members of the deal team have maintained a neutral perspective regarding the acquisition. If they have become emotional about it, the remedy, again, is to examine with extra thoroughness all the components of the recommendation and all the biases that may have affected the people making it.

3. Were there dissenting opinions within the recommending team? If so, were they explored adequately? In many corporate cultures, a team presenting a recommendation to a higher echelon will claim to be unanimous. The unanimity is sometimes genuine, but it could be sham unity imposed by the team's leader or a case of groupthink—the tendency of groups to minimize conflict by converging on a decision because it appears to be gathering support. Groupthink is especially likely if there is little diversity of background and viewpoint within a team. Lisa, for instance, should worry if no one in the manufacturing team that is proposing the large investment has voiced any concerns or disagreement.

Regardless of its cause, an absence of dissent in a team addressing a complex problem should sound an alarm. In the long run, a senior executive should strive to create a climate where substantive disagreements are seen as a productive part of the decision process (and resolved objectively), rather than as a sign of conflict between individuals (and suppressed). In the short run, if faced with a recommendation in which dissent clearly was stifled, a decision maker has few options. Because asking another group of people to generate additional options is often impractical, the best choice may be to discreetly solicit dissenting views from members of the recommending team, perhaps through private meetings. And the opinions of those who braved the pressure for conformity in the decision-making process deserve special attention.

Questions that decision makers should ask the team making recommendations

4. Could the diagnosis of the situation be overly influenced by salient analogies? Many recommendations refer to a past success story, which the decision maker is encouraged to repeat by approving the proposal. The business development team advocating the acquisition to Devesh took this approach, using the example of a recent successful deal it had completed to bolster its case. The danger, of course, is that the analogy may be less relevant to the current deal than it appears. Furthermore, the use of just one or a few analogies almost always leads to faulty inferences.

The decision maker who suspects that an analogy to an especially memorable event has unduly influenced a team's judgment (a type of cognitive flaw known as *saliency bias*) will want the team to explore alternative diagnoses. This can be done by asking for more analogies and a rigorous analysis of how comparable examples really are. (For more details on the technique for doing this, called *reference class forecasting*, see "Delusions of Success: How Optimism Undermines Executives' Decisions," by Dan Lovallo and Daniel Kahneman, HBR July 2003.) More informally, a decision maker can simply prompt the team to use a broader set of comparisons. Devesh could ask for descriptions of five recent deals, other than the recently acquired company, that were somewhat similar to the one being considered.

5. Have credible alternatives been considered? In a good decision process, other alternatives are fully evaluated in an objective and fact-based way. Yet when trying to solve a problem, both individuals and groups are prone to generating one plausible hypothesis and then seeking only evidence that supports it.

A good practice is to insist that people submit at least one or two alternatives to the main recommendation and explain their pros and cons. A decision maker should ask: What alternatives did you consider? At what stage were they discarded? Did you actively look for information that would disprove your main hypothesis or only for the confirming evidence described in your final recommendation?

Some proposals feature a perfunctory list of "risks and mitigating actions" or a set of implausible alternatives that make the recommendation look appealing by contrast. The challenge is to encourage a *genuine* admission of uncertainty and a sincere recognition of multiple options.

In his review, Bob should encourage his sales colleagues to recognize the unknowns surrounding their proposal. The team may eventually admit that competitors' reactions to an across-the-board price cut are unpredictable. It should then be willing to evaluate other options, such as a targeted marketing program aimed at the customer segments in which Bob's company has a competitive advantage.

6. If you had to make this decision again in a year, what information would you want, and can you get more of it now? One challenge executives face when reviewing a recommendation is the WYSIATI assumption: What you see is all there is. Because our intuitive mind constructs a coherent narrative based on the evidence we have, making up for holes in it, we tend to overlook what is missing. Devesh, for instance, found the acquisition proposal compelling until he realized he had not seen a legal due diligence on the target company's patent portfolio—perhaps not a major issue if the acquisition were being made primarily to gain new customers but a critical question when the goal was to extend the product line.

To force yourself to examine the adequacy of the data, Harvard Business School professor Max Bazerman suggests asking the question above. In many cases, data are unavailable. But in some cases, useful information will be uncovered.

Checklists that specify what information is relevant to a certain type of decision are also helpful. Devesh, for his part, could tap his experience reviewing acquisition proposals and develop lists of data that should be collected for each different kind of deal his company does, such as acquiring new technology or buying access to new customers.

7. Do you know where the numbers came from? A focused examination of the key numbers underlying the proposal will help decision makers see through any anchoring bias. Questions to ask include: Which numbers in this plan are facts and which are estimates? Were these estimates developed by adjusting from another number? Who put the first number on the table?

Three different types of anchoring bias are common in business decisions. In the classic case, initial estimates, which are often best guesses, are used, and their accuracy is not challenged. The team making the proposal to Lisa, for instance, used a guesstimate on an important cost component of the capital investment project. More frequently, estimates are based on extrapolations from history, as they were when Devesh's team predicted the target company's sales by drawing a straight line. This, too, is a form of anchoring bias; one cannot always assume trends will continue. Finally, some anchors are clearly deliberate, such as when a buyer sets a low floor in a price negotiation. The trap of anchors is that people always believe they can disregard them, but in fact they cannot. Judges who are asked to roll a set of dice before making a (fortunately simulated) sentencing decision will of course deny that the dice influenced them, but analysis of their decisions shows that they did.

When a recommendation appears to be anchored by an initial reference and the number in question has a material impact, the decision maker should require the team behind the proposal to adjust its estimates after some reanchoring. If Lisa discovers that the investment budget she was asked to approve was derived from the costing of an earlier project, she can reanchor the team with a number she arrives at in a completely different way, such as a linear model based on investment projects carried out in other divisions, or competitive benchmarks. The aim is neither to arrive directly at a different number nor to slavishly "copy and paste" the practices of benchmarked competitors, but to force the team to consider its assumptions in another light.

8. Can you see a *halo effect*? This effect is at work when we see a story as simpler and more emotionally coherent than it really is. As Phil Rosenzweig shows in the book *The Halo Effect,* it causes us to attribute the successes and failures of firms to the personalities of their leaders. It may have led Devesh's team to link the success of the acquisition target to its senior management and assume that its recent outperformance would continue as long as those managers were still in place.

Companies deemed "excellent" are frequently circled by halos. Once an expert brands them in this way, people tend to assume that all their practices must be exemplary. In making its case for its capital investment, Lisa's team, for instance, pointed to a similar project undertaken by a highly admired company in another cyclical industry. According to the proposal, that company had "doubled down" on a moderately successful manufacturing investment, which paid off when the economy rebounded and the extra capacity was fully used.

Naturally, Lisa should ask whether the inference is justified. Does the team making the recommendation have specific information regarding the other company's decision, or is the team making assumptions based on the company's overall reputation? If the investment was indeed a success, how much of that success is attributable to chance events such as lucky timing? And is the situation of the other company truly similar to the situation of Lisa's company?

Such difficult questions are rarely asked, in part because it may seem off-base to take apart an outside comparison that is made in passing. Yet if Lisa simply tries to disregard the comparison, she will still be left with a vague, but hard to dispel, positive impression of the recommendation. A good and relatively simple practice is to first assess the relevance of the comparison ("What about this case is comparable with ours?") and then ask the people making it to propose other examples from less successful companies ("What other companies in our industry invested in a declining business, and how did it turn out for them?").

9. Are the people making the recommendation overly attached to past decisions? Companies do not start from scratch every day. Their history, and what they learn from it, matter. But history leads us astray when we evaluate options in reference to a past starting point instead of the future. The most visible consequence is the *sunk-cost fallacy*: When considering new investments, we should disregard past expenditures that don't affect future costs or revenues, but we don't. Note that Lisa's team was evaluating a capacity improvement in a product line that was struggling financially—partly because it was subscale, the team argued. Lisa should ask the team to look at this investment the way an incoming CEO might: If I personally hadn't decided to build the plant in the first place, would I invest in adding capacity?

Questions focused on evaluating the proposal

10. Is the base case overly optimistic? Most recommendations contain forecasts, which are notoriously prone to excessive optimism. One contributing factor is overconfidence, which could, say, lead Devesh's team to underestimate the challenge of integrating the acquired company and capturing synergies. Groups with a successful track record are more prone to this bias than others, so Devesh should be especially careful if the business development team has been on a winning streak.

Another factor frequently at work here is the *planning fallacy*. The planning fallacy arises from "inside view" thinking, which focuses exclusively on the case at hand and ignores the history of similar projects. This is like trying to divine the future of a company by considering only its plans and the obstacles it anticipates. An "outside view" of forecasting, in contrast, is statistical in nature and mainly uses the generalizable aspects of a broad set of problems to make predictions. Lisa should keep this in mind when reviewing her team's proposal. When drawing up a timeline for the completion of the proposed plant, did the team use a top-down (outside-view) comparison with similar projects, or did it estimate the time

Improving Decisions Throughout the Organization

To critique recommendations effectively and in a sustainable way, you need to make quality control more than an individual effort.

Organizations pursue this objective in various ways, but good approaches have three principles in common. First, they adopt the right mind-set. The goal is not to create bureaucratic procedures or turn decision quality control into another element of "compliance" that can be delegated to a risk assessment unit. It's to stimulate discussion and debate. To accomplish this, organizations must tolerate and even encourage disagreements (as long as they are based on facts and not personal).

Second, they rotate the people in charge, rather than rely on one executive to be the quality policeman. Many companies, at least in theory, expect a functional leader such as a CFO or a chief strategy officer to play the role of challenger. But an insider whose primary job is to critique others loses political capital quickly. The use of a quality checklist may reduce this downside, as the challenger will be seen as "only playing by the rules," but high-quality debate is still unlikely.

Third, they inject a diversity of views and a mix of skills into the process. Some firms form ad hoc critique teams, asking outsiders or employees rotating in from other divisions to review plans. One company calls them "provocateurs" and makes playing this role a stage of leadership development. Another, as part of its strategic planning, systematically organizes critiques and brings in outside experts to do them. Both companies have explicitly thought about their decision processes, particularly those involving strategic plans, and invested effort in honing them. They have made their decision processes a source of competitive advantage.

---

required for each step and add it up—a bottom-up (inside-view) approach that is likely to result in underestimates?

A third factor is the failure to anticipate how competitors will respond to a decision. For instance, in proposing price cuts, Bob's team did not account for the predictable reaction of the company's competitors: starting a price war.

All these biases are exacerbated in most organizations by the inevitable interplay (and frequent confusion) between forecasts and estimates on the one hand, and plans or targets on the other.

Forecasts should be accurate, whereas targets should be ambitious. The two sets of numbers should not be confused by senior leadership. Correcting for optimistic biases is difficult, and asking teams to revise their estimates will not suffice. The decision maker must take the lead by adopting an outside view, as opposed to the inside view of the people making proposals.

Several techniques help promote an outside view. Lisa could construct a list of several similar investment projects and ask her team to look at how long those projects took to complete, thus removing from the equation all inside information on the project at hand. Sometimes, removing what appears to be valuable information yields better estimates. In some situations decision makers might also put themselves in the shoes of their competitors. The use of "war games" is a powerful antidote to the lack of thinking about competitors' reactions to proposed moves.

11. Is the worst case bad enough? Many companies, when making important decisions, ask strategy teams to propose a range of scenarios, or at least a best and a worst case. Unfortunately, the worst case is rarely bad enough. A decision maker should ask: Where did the worst case come from? How sensitive is it to our competitors' responses? What could happen that we have not thought of?

The acquisition proposal Devesh is reviewing hinges on the target's sales forecast, and like most sales forecasts in due diligence reports, it follows a steep, straight, upward line. Devesh may ask his team to prepare a range of scenarios reflecting the merger's risks, but the team is likely to miss risks it has not experienced yet.

A useful technique in such situations is the "premortem," pioneered by psychologist Gary Klein. Participants project themselves into the future, imagine the worst has already happened, and make up a story about how it happened. Devesh's team could consider such scenarios as the departure of key executives who do not fit into the acquiring company's culture, technical problems with the target's key product lines, and insufficient resources for integration. It would then be able to consider whether to mitigate those risks or reassess the proposal.

12. Is the recommending team overly cautious? On the flip side, excessive conservatism is a source of less visible but serious chronic underperformance in organizations. Many executives complain that their teams' plans aren't creative or ambitious enough.

This issue is hard to address for two reasons. First and most important, the people making recommendations are subject to loss aversion: When they contemplate risky decisions, their wish to avoid losses is stronger than their desire for gains. No individual or team wants to be responsible for a failed project. Second, the fact that very few companies make explicit choices about what level of risk they will assume only exacerbates individual managers' loss aversion.

This helps explain why Lisa's colleagues had ruled out a new technology providing an alternative to the proposed investment: They deemed it too risky. To get her team to explore this option, she could provide assurances or (perhaps more credibly) explicitly share responsibility for the risk. When launching new ventures, many companies tackle this problem by creating separate organizational units with different objectives and budgets. But dealing with excessive conservatism in "ordinary" operations remains a challenge.

Implementing Quality Control Over Decisions

These 12 questions should be helpful to anyone who relies substantially on others' evaluations to make a final decision. But there's a time and place to ask them, and there are ways to make them part and parcel of your organization's decision-making processes.

When to use the Checklist
This approach is not designed for routine decisions that an executive formally rubber-stamps. Lisa, the CFO, will want to use it for major capital expenditures but not her department's operating budget. The sweet spot for quality control is decisions that are both important and recurring, and so justify a formal process. Approving an R&D project, deciding on a large capital expenditure, and making a midsize acquisition of a company are all examples of "quality controllable" decisions.

Who should conduct the review

As we mentioned earlier, the very idea of quality control also assumes a real separation between the decision maker and the team making the recommendation. In many instances an executive will overtly or covertly influence a team's proposal, perhaps by picking team members whose opinions are already known, making his or her preferences clear in advance, or signaling opinions during the recommendation phase. If that is the case, the decision maker becomes a de facto member of the recommendation team and can no longer judge the quality of the proposal because his or her own biases have influenced it.

A clear and common sign that this has happened is overlap between the decision and action stages. If, at the time of a decision, steps have already been taken to implement it, the executive making the final call has probably communicated a preference for the outcome being recommended.

Enforcing discipline

Last, executives need to be prepared to be systematic—something that not all corporate cultures welcome. As Atul Gawande points out in *The Checklist Manifesto,* because each item on a checklist tends to seem sensible and unsurprising, it is tempting to use checklists partially and selectively. Doctors who adopted the World Health Organization's Surgical Safety Checklist knew that measures as simple as checking the patient's medication allergies made sense. But only by going through the checklist completely, systematically, and routinely did they achieve results—a spectacular reduction in complications and mortality. Using checklists is a matter of discipline, not genius. Partial adherence may be a recipe for total failure.

Costs and benefits

Is applying quality control to decisions a good investment of effort? Time-pressed executives do not want to delay action, and few corporations are prepared to devote special resources to a quality control exercise.

But in the end, Bob, Lisa, and Devesh all did, and averted serious problems as a result. Bob resisted the temptation to implement the price cut his team was clamoring for at the risk of destroying profitability and triggering a price war. Instead, he challenged the team to propose an alternative, and eventually successful, marketing plan. Lisa refused to approve an investment that, as she discovered, aimed to justify and prop up earlier sunk-cost investments in the same business. Her team later proposed an investment in a new technology that would leapfrog the competition. Finally, Devesh signed off on the deal his team was proposing, but not before additional due diligence had uncovered issues that led to a significant reduction in the acquisition price.

The real challenge for executives who want to implement decision quality control is not time or cost. It is the need to build awareness that even highly experienced, superbly competent, and well-intentioned managers are fallible. Organizations need to realize that a disciplined decision-making process, not individual genius, is the key to a sound strategy. And they will have to create a culture of open debate in which such processes can flourish.

Originally published in June 2011. Reprint R1106B

How to Avoid Catastrophe

Failures happen. But if you pay attention to near misses, you can predict and prevent crises.

by Catherine H. Tinsley, Robin L. Dillon, and Peter M. Madsen

MOST PEOPLE THINK OF "near misses" as harrowing close calls that could have been a lot worse—when a firefighter escapes a burning building moments before it collapses, or when a tornado miraculously veers away from a town in its path. Events like these are rare narrow escapes that leave us shaken and looking for lessons.

But there's another class of near misses, ones that are much more common and pernicious. These are the often unremarked small failures that permeate day-to-day business but cause no immediate harm. People are hardwired to misinterpret or ignore the warnings embedded in these failures, and so they often go unexamined or, perversely, are seen as signs that systems are resilient and things are going well. Yet these seemingly innocuous events are often harbingers; if conditions shift slightly, or if luck does not intervene, a crisis erupts.

Consider the BP Gulf oil rig disaster. As a case study in the anatomy of near misses and the consequences of misreading them, it's close to perfect. In April 2010, a gas blowout occurred during the cementing of the *Deepwater Horizon* well. The blowout ignited, killing 11 people, sinking the rig, and triggering a massive underwater spill that would take months to contain. Numerous poor decisions and dangerous conditions contributed to the disaster: Drillers had used too few centralizers to position the pipe, the lubricating "drilling mud" was removed too early, managers had misinterpreted vital test results that would have confirmed that hydrocarbons were seeping from the well. In addition, BP relied on an older version of a complex fail-safe device called a blowout preventer that had a notoriously spotty track record.

Why did Transocean (the rig's owner), BP executives, rig managers, and the drilling crew overlook the warning signs, even though the well had been plagued by technical problems all along (crew members called it "the well from hell")? We believe that the stakeholders were lulled into complacency by a catalog of previous near misses in the industry—successful outcomes in which luck played a key role in averting disaster. Increasing numbers of ultradeep wells were being drilled, but significant oil spills or fatalities were extremely rare. And many Gulf of Mexico wells had suffered minor blowouts during cementing (dozens of them in the past two decades); however, in each case chance factors—favorable wind direction, no one welding near the leak at the time, for instance—helped prevent an explosion. Each near miss, rather than raise alarms and prompt investigations, was taken as an indication that existing methods and safety procedures worked.

For the past seven years, we have studied near misses in dozens of companies across industries from telecommunications to automobiles, at NASA, and in lab simulations. Our research reveals a pattern: Multiple near misses preceded (and foreshadowed) every disaster and business crisis we studied, and most of the misses were ignored or misread. Our work also shows that cognitive biases conspire to blind managers to the near misses. Two in particular cloud our judgment. The first is "normalization of deviance," the tendency over time to accept anomalies—particularly risky ones—as normal. Think of the growing comfort a worker might feel with using a ladder with a broken rung; the more times he climbs the dangerous ladder without incident, the safer he feels it is. For an organization, such normalization can be catastrophic. Columbia University sociologist

Idea in Brief

Most business failures—such as engineering disasters, product malfunctions, and PR crises—are foreshadowed by near misses, close calls that, had luck not intervened, would have had far worse consequences. The space shuttle Columbia's fatal reentry, BP's Gulf oil rig disaster, Toyota's stuck accelerators, even the iPhone 4's antenna failures—all were preceded by near-miss events that should have tipped off managers to impending crises. The problem is that near misses are often overlooked—or, perversely, viewed as a sign that systems are resilient and working well. That's because managers are blinded by cognitive biases, argue Georgetown professors Tinsley and Dillon and Brigham Young University's Madsen. Seven strategies can help managers recognize and learn from near misses: They should be on increased alert when time or cost pressures are high; watch for deviations in operations from the norm and uncover their root causes; make decision makers accountable for near misses; envision worst-case scenarios; be on the lookout for near-misses masquerading as successes; and reward individuals for exposing near misses.

Diane Vaughan coined the phrase in her book *The Challenger Launch Decision* to describe the organizational behaviors that allowed a glaring mechanical anomaly on the space shuttle to gradually be viewed as a normal flight risk—dooming its crew. The second cognitive error is the so-called outcome bias. When people observe successful outcomes, they tend to focus on the results more than on the (often unseen) complex processes that led to them.

Recognizing and learning from near misses isn't simply a matter of paying attention; it actually runs contrary to human nature. In this article, we examine near misses and reveal how companies can detect and learn from them. By seeing them for what they are—instructive failures—managers can apply their lessons to improve operations and, potentially, ward off catastrophe.

Roots of Crises

Consider this revealing experiment: We asked business students, NASA personnel, and space-industry contractors to evaluate a fictional project manager, Chris, who was supervising the launch

Focus on failure

"Every strike brings me closer to the next home run."

Babe Ruth
Baseball player

of an unmanned spacecraft and had made a series of decisions, including skipping the investigation of a potential design flaw and forgoing a peer review, because of time pressure. Each participant was given one of three scenarios: The spacecraft launched without issue and was able to transmit data (success outcome); shortly after launch, the spacecraft had a problem caused by the design flaw, but because of the way the sun happened to be aligned with the vehicle it was still able to transmit data (near-miss outcome); or the craft had a problem caused by the flaw and, because of the sun's chance alignment, it failed to transmit data and was lost (failure outcome).

How did Chris fare? Participants were just as likely to praise his decision making, leadership abilities, and the overall mission in the success case as in the near-miss case—though the latter plainly succeeded only because of blind luck. When people observe a successful outcome, their natural tendency is to assume that the process that led to it was fundamentally sound, even when it demonstrably wasn't; hence the common phrase "you can't argue with success." In fact, you can—and should.

Organizational disasters, studies show, rarely have a single cause. Rather, they are initiated by the unexpected interaction of multiple small, often seemingly unimportant, human errors, technological failures, or bad business decisions. These latent errors combine with enabling conditions to produce a significant failure. A latent error on an oil rig might be a cementing procedure that allows gas to escape; enabling conditions might be a windless day and a welder working near the leak. Together, the latent error and enabling conditions ignite a deadly firestorm. Near misses arise from the same preconditions, but in the absence of enabling conditions, they produce only small failures and thus go undetected or are ignored.

Latent errors often exist for long periods of time before they combine with enabling conditions to produce a significant failure. Whether an enabling condition transforms a near miss into a crisis generally depends on chance; thus, it makes little sense to try to predict or control enabling conditions. Instead, companies should focus on identifying and fixing latent errors before circumstances allow them to create a crisis.

Oil rig explosions offer a dramatic case in point, but latent errors and enabling conditions in business often combine to produce less spectacular but still costly crises—corporate failures that attention to latent errors could have prevented. Let's look at three.

Bad Apple

Take Apple's experience following its launch of the iPhone 4, in June 2010. Almost immediately, customers began complaining about dropped calls and poor signal strength. Apple's initial response was to blame users for holding the phone the wrong way, thus covering

---

Focus on failure

Wages
U.S. productivity grew at a healthy clip from 1973 to 2009. Median wages didn't come close to matching those gains.

Productivity

Median family income

'47 '51 '55 '59 '63 '67 '71 '75 '79 '83 '87 '91 '95 '99 '03 '07

Source: Economic Policy Institute

45

the external antenna, and to advise them to "avoid gripping [the phone] in the lower left corner." When questioned about the problem by a user on a web forum, CEO Steve Jobs fired back an e-mail describing the dropped calls as a "non issue." Many customers found Apple's posture arrogant and insulting and made their displeasure known through social and mainstream media. Several filed class action lawsuits, including a suit that alleged "fraud by concealment, negligence, intentional misrepresentation and defective design." The reputation crisis reached a crescendo in mid-July, when *Consumer Reports* declined to recommend the iPhone 4 (it had recommended all previous versions). Ultimately Apple backpedaled, acknowledging software errors and offering owners software updates and iPhone cases to address the antenna problem.

The latent errors underlying the crisis had long been present. As Jobs demonstrated during a press conference, virtually all smartphones experience a drop in signal strength when users touch the external antenna. This flaw had existed in earlier iPhones, as well as in competitors' phones, for years. The phones' signal strength problem was also well known. Other latent errors emerged as the crisis gained momentum, notably an evasive PR strategy that invited a backlash.

That consumers had endured the performance issues for years without significant comment was not a sign of a successful strategy but of an ongoing near miss. When coupled with the right enabling conditions—*Consumer Reports'* withering and widely quoted review and the expanding reach of social media—a crisis erupted. If Apple had recognized consumers' forbearance as an ongoing near miss and proactively fixed the phones' technical problems, it could have avoided the crisis. It didn't, we suspect, because of normalization bias, which made the antenna glitch seem increasingly acceptable; and because of outcome bias, which led managers to conclude that the lack of outcry about the phones' shortcomings reflected their own good strategy—rather than good luck.

Speed warning
On August 28, 2009, California Highway Patrol officer Mark Saylor and three family members died in a fiery crash after the gas pedal of

the Lexus sedan they were driving in stuck, accelerating the car to more than 120 miles per hour. A 911 call from the speeding car captured the horrifying moments before the crash and was replayed widely in the news and social media.

Up to this point, Toyota, which makes Lexus, had downplayed the more than 2,000 complaints of unintended acceleration among its cars it had received since 2001. The Saylor tragedy forced the company to seriously investigate the problem. Ultimately, Toyota recalled more than 6 million vehicles in late 2009 and early 2010 and temporarily halted production and sales of eight models, sustaining an estimated $2 billion loss in North American sales alone and immeasurable harm to its reputation.

Complaints about vehicle acceleration and speed control are common for all automakers, and in most cases, according to the National Highway Traffic Safety Administration, the problems are

Toyota pedal problems

Errors in process or product design are often ignored, even when the warning signs clearly call for action. The more times small failures occur without disaster, the more complacent managers become.

Percentage of customer complaints having to do with speed control

Source: National Highway Traffic Safety Administration

caused by driver error, not a vehicle defect. However, beginning in 2001, about the time that Toyota introduced a new accelerator design, complaints of acceleration problems in Toyotas increased sharply, whereas such complaints remained relatively constant for other automakers (see the exhibit "Toyota pedal problems"). Toyota could have averted the crisis if it had noted this deviation and acknowledged the thousands of complaints for what they were—near misses. Here, too, normalization of deviance and outcome bias, along with other factors, conspired to obscure the grave implications of the near misses. Only when an enabling condition occurred—the Saylor family tragedy and the ensuing media storm—did the latent error trigger a crisis.

Jet Black and Blue

Since it began operating, in 2000, JetBlue Airways has taken an aggressive approach to bad weather, canceling proportionately fewer flights than other airlines and directing its pilots to pull away from gates as soon as possible in severe weather so as to be near the front of the line when runways were cleared for takeoff—even if that meant loaded planes would sit for some time on the tarmac. For several years, this policy seemed to work. On-tarmac delays were not arduously long, and customers were by and large accepting of them. Nonetheless, it was a risky strategy, exposing the airline to the danger of stranding passengers for extended periods if conditions abruptly worsened.

The wake-up call came on February 14, 2007. A massive ice storm at New York's John F. Kennedy International Airport caused widespread disruption—but no carrier was harder hit than JetBlue, whose assertive pilots now found themselves stuck on the tarmac (literally, in some cases, because of frozen wheels) and with no open gates to return to. Distressed passengers on several planes were trapped for up to 11 hours in overheated, foul-smelling cabins with little food or water. The media served up angry first-person accounts of the ordeal, and a chastened David Neeleman, JetBlue's CEO, acknowledged on CNBC, "We did a horrible job, actually, of getting

JetBlue tarmac trouble

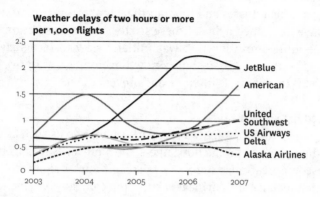

Weather delays of two hours or more per 1,000 flights

Source: Department of Transportation's Bureau of Transportation Statistics

our customers off those airplanes." The airline reported canceling more than 250 of its 505 flights that day—a much higher proportion than any other airline. It lost millions of dollars and squandered priceless consumer loyalty.

For JetBlue, each of the thousands of flights that took off before the competition during previous weather delays was a near miss. As the airline continued to get away with the risky strategy, managers who had expressed concern early on about the way the airline handled flight delays became complacent, even as long delays mounted. Indeed, the proportion of JetBlue weather-based delays of two hours or more roughly tripled between 2003 and 2007, whereas such delays remained fairly steady at other major U.S. airlines (see the exhibit "JetBlue tarmac trouble").

Rather than perceiving that a dramatic increase in delays represented a dramatic increase in risk, JetBlue managers saw only successfully launched flights. It took an enabling condition—the ferocious ice storm—to turn the latent error into a crisis.

Recognizing and Preventing Near Misses

Our research suggests seven strategies that can help organizations recognize near misses and root out the latent errors behind them. We have developed many of these strategies in collaboration with NASA—an organization that was initially slow to recognize the relevance of near misses but is now developing enterprisewide programs to identify, learn from, and prevent them.

1. Heed high pressure

The greater the pressure to meet performance goals such as tight schedules, cost, or production targets, the more likely managers are to discount near-miss signals or misread them as signs of sound decision making. BP's managers knew the company was incurring overrun costs of $1 million a day in rig lease and contractor fees, which surely contributed to their failure to recognize warning signs.

The high-pressure effect also contributed to the *Columbia* space shuttle disaster, in which insulation foam falling from the external fuel tank damaged the shuttle's wing during liftoff, causing the shuttle to break apart as it reentered the atmosphere. Managers had been aware of the foam issue since the start of the shuttle program and were concerned about it early on, but as dozens of flights proceeded without serious mishap, they began to classify foam strikes as maintenance issues—rather than as near misses. This classic case of normalization of deviance was exacerbated by the enormous political pressure the agency was under at the time to complete the International Space Station's main core. Delays on the shuttle, managers knew, would slow down the space station project.

Despite renewed concern about foam strikes caused by a particularly dramatic recent near miss, and with an investigation under way, the *Columbia* took off. According to the Columbia Accident Investigation Board, "The pressure of maintaining the flight schedule created a management atmosphere that increasingly accepted less-than-specification performance of various components and systems."

When people make decisions under pressure, psychological research shows, they tend to rely on heuristics, or rules of thumb, and thus are more easily influenced by biases. In high-pressure work environments, managers should expect people to be more easily swayed by outcome bias, more likely to normalize deviance, and more apt to believe that their decisions are sound. Organizations should encourage, or even require, employees to examine their decisions during pressure-filled periods and ask, "If I had more time and resources, would I make the same decision?"

2. Learn from deviations

As the Toyota and JetBlue crises suggest, managers' response when some aspect of operations skews from the norm is often to recalibrate what they consider acceptable risk. Our research shows that in such cases, decision makers may clearly understand the statistical risk represented by the deviation, but grow increasingly less concerned about it.

We've seen this effect clearly in a laboratory setting. Turning again to the space program for insight, we asked study participants to assume operational control of a Mars rover in a simulated mission. Each morning they received a weather report and had to decide whether or not to drive onward. On the second day, they learned that there was a 95% chance of a severe sandstorm, which had a 40% chance of causing catastrophic wheel failure. Half the participants were told that the rover had successfully driven through sandstorms in the past (that is, it had emerged unscathed in several prior near misses); the other half had no information about the rover's luck in past storms. When the time came to choose whether or not to risk the drive, three quarters of the near-miss group opted to continue driving; only 13% of the other group did. Both groups knew, and indeed stated that they knew, that the risk of failure was 40%—but the near-miss group was much more comfortable with that level of risk.

Managers should seek out operational deviations from the norm and examine whether their reasons for tolerating the associated risk have merit. Questions to ask might be: Have we always been comfortable with this level of risk? Has our policy toward this risk changed over time?

3. Uncover root causes

When managers identify deviations, their reflex is often to correct the symptom rather than its cause. Such was Apple's response when it at first suggested that customers address the antenna problem by changing the way they held the iPhone. NASA learned this lesson the hard way as well, during its 1998 Mars Climate Orbiter mission. As the spacecraft headed toward Mars it drifted slightly off course four times; each time, managers made small trajectory adjustments, but they didn't investigate the cause of the drifting. As the $200 million spacecraft approached Mars, instead of entering into orbit, it disintegrated in the atmosphere. Only then did NASA uncover the latent error—programmers had used English rather than metric units in their software coding. The course corrections addressed the symptom of the problem but not the underlying cause. Their apparent success lulled decision makers into thinking that the issue had been adequately resolved.

The health care industry has made great strides in learning from near misses and offers a model for others. Providers are increasingly encouraged to report mistakes and near misses so that the lessons can be teased out and applied. An article in *Today's Hospitalist,* for example, describes a near miss at Delnor-Community Hospital, in Geneva, Illinois. Two patients sharing a hospital room had similar last names and were prescribed drugs with similar-sounding names—Cytotec and Cytoxan. Confused by the similarities, a nurse nearly administered one of the drugs to the wrong patient. Luckily, she caught her mistake in time and filed a report detailing the close call. The hospital immediately separated the patients and created a policy to prevent patients with similar names from sharing rooms in the future.

4. Demand accountability

Even when people are aware of near misses, they tend to downgrade their importance. One way to limit this potentially dangerous effect is to require managers to justify their assessments of near misses.

Remember Chris, the fictional manager in our study who neglected some due diligence in his supervision of a space mission? Par-

Little Near Misses and Small-Scale Failures

We've used dramatic cases such as oil spills and shuttle disasters to illustrate how near misses can foreshadow huge calamities.

But near misses are relevant to managers at all levels in their day-to-day work, as they can also presage lesser but still consequential problems. Research on workplace safety, for example, estimates that for every 1,000 near misses, one accident results in a serious injury or fatality, at least 10 smaller accidents cause minor injuries, and 30 cause property damage but no injury. Identifying near misses and addressing the latent errors that give rise to them can head off the more mundane problems that distract organizations and sap their resources.

Imagine an associate who misses deadlines and is chronically late for client meetings but is otherwise a high performer. Each tardy project and late arrival is a near miss; but by addressing the symptoms of the problem—covering for the employee in a variety of ways—his manager is able to prevent clients from defecting. By doing this, however, she permits a small but significant erosion of client satisfaction, team cohesiveness, and organizational performance. And eventually, a client may jump ship—an outcome that could have been avoided by attending to the near misses. Your organization needn't face a threat as serious as an oil spill to benefit from exposing near misses of all types and addressing their root causes.

---

ticipants gave him equally good marks for the success scenario and the near-miss scenario. Chris's raters didn't seem to see that the near miss was in fact a near disaster. In a continuation of that study, we told a separate group of managers and contractors that they would have to justify their assessment of Chris to upper management. Knowing they'd have to explain their rating to the bosses, those evaluating the near-miss scenario judged Chris's performance just as harshly as did those who had learned the mission had failed—recognizing, it seems, that rather than managing well, he'd simply dodged a bullet.

5. Consider worst-case scenarios
Unless expressly advised to do so, people tend not to think through the possible negative consequences of near misses. Apple managers,

for example, were aware of the iPhone's antenna problems but probably hadn't imagined how bad a consumer backlash could get. If they had considered a worst-case scenario, they might have headed off the crisis, our research suggests.

In one study, we told participants to suppose that an impending hurricane had a 30% chance of hitting their house and asked them if they would evacuate. Just as in our Mars rover study, people who were told that they'd escaped disaster in previous near misses were more likely to take a chance (in this case, opting to stay home). However, when we told participants to suppose that, although their house had survived previous hurricanes, a neighbor's house had been hit by a tree during one, they saw things differently; this group was far more likely to evacuate. Examining events closely helps people distinguish between near misses and successes, and they'll often adjust their decision making accordingly.

Managers in Walmart's business-continuity office clearly understand this. For several years prior to Hurricane Katrina, the office had carefully evaluated previous hurricane near misses of its stores and infrastructure and, based on them, planned for a direct hit to a metro area where it had a large presence. In the days before Katrina made landfall in Louisiana, the company expanded the staff of its emergency command center from the usual six to 10 people to more than 50, and stockpiled food, water, and emergency supplies in its local warehouses. Having learned from prior near misses, Walmart famously outperformed local and federal officials in responding to the disaster. Said Jefferson Parish sheriff Harry Lee, "If the American government had responded like Walmart has responded, we wouldn't be in this crisis."

6. Evaluate projects at every stage

When things go badly, managers commonly conduct postmortems to determine causes and prevent recurrences. When they go well, however, few do formal reviews of the success to capture its lessons. Because near misses can look like successes, they often escape scrutiny.

The chief knowledge officer at NASA's Goddard Space Flight Center, Edward Rogers, instituted a "pause and learn" process in which teams discuss at each project milestone what they have learned. They not only cover mishaps but also expressly examine perceived successes and the design decisions considered along the way. By critically examining projects while they're under way, teams avoid outcome bias and are more likely to see near misses for what they are. These sessions are followed by knowledge-sharing workshops involving a broader group of teams. Other NASA centers, including the Jet Propulsion Laboratory, which manages NASA's Mars program, are beginning similar experiments. According to Rogers, most projects that have used the pause-and-learn process have uncovered near misses—typically, design flaws that had gone undetected. "Almost every mishap at NASA can be traced to some series of small signals that went unnoticed at the critical moment," he says.

7. Reward owning up

Seeing and attending to near misses requires organizational alertness, but no amount of attention will avert failure if people aren't motivated to expose near misses—or, worse, are discouraged from doing so. In many organizations, employees have reason to keep quiet about failures, and in that type of environment they're likely to keep suspicions about near misses to themselves.

Political scientists Martin Landau and Donald Chisholm described one such case that, though it took place on the deck of a warship, is relevant to any organization. An enlisted seaman on an aircraft carrier discovered during a combat exercise that he'd lost a tool on the deck. He knew that an errant tool could cause a catastrophe if it were sucked into a jet engine, and he was also aware that admitting the mistake could bring a halt to the exercise—and potential punishment. As long as the tool was unaccounted for, each successful takeoff and landing would be a near miss, a lucky outcome. He reported the mistake, the exercise was stopped, and all aircraft aloft were redirected to bases on land, at a significant cost.

Rather than being punished for his error, the seaman was commended by his commanding officer in a formal ceremony for his bravery in reporting it. Leaders in any organization should publicly reward staff for uncovering near misses—including their own.

Two Forces conspire to make learning from near misses difficult: Cognitive biases make them hard to see, and, even when they are visible, leaders tend not to grasp their significance. Thus, organizations often fail to expose and correct latent errors even when the cost of doing so is small—and so they miss opportunities for organizational improvement before disaster strikes. This tendency is itself a type of organizational failure—a failure to learn from "cheap" data. Surfacing near misses and correcting root causes is one of the soundest investments an organization can make.

Originally published in April 2011. Reprint R1104G

Conquering a Culture of Indecision

by Ram Charan

DOES THIS SOUND FAMILIAR? You're sitting in the quarterly business review as a colleague plows through a two-inch-thick proposal for a big investment in a new product. When he finishes, the room falls quiet. People look left, right, or down, waiting for someone else to open the discussion. No one wants to comment—at least not until the boss shows which way he's leaning.

Finally, the CEO breaks the loud silence. He asks a few mildly skeptical questions to show he's done his due diligence. But it's clear that he has made up his mind to back the project. Before long, the other meeting attendees are chiming in dutifully, careful to keep their comments positive. Judging from the remarks, it appears that everyone in the room supports the project.

But appearances can be deceiving. The head of a related division worries that the new product will take resources away from his operation. The vice president of manufacturing thinks that the first-year sales forecasts are wildly optimistic and will leave him with a warehouse full of unsold goods. Others in the room are lukewarm because they don't see how they stand to gain from the project. But they keep their reservations to themselves, and the meeting breaks up inconclusively. Over the next few months, the project is slowly strangled to death in a series of strategy, budget, and operational reviews. It's not clear who's responsible for the killing, but it's plain that the true sentiment in the room was the opposite of the apparent consensus.

In my career as an adviser to large organizations and their leaders, I have witnessed many occasions even at the highest levels when silent lies and a lack of closure lead to false decisions. They are "false" because they eventually get undone by unspoken factors and inaction. And after a quarter century of first-hand observations, I have concluded that these instances of indecision share a family resemblance—a misfire in the personal interactions that are supposed to produce results. The people charged with reaching a decision and acting on it fail to connect and engage with one another. Intimidated by the group dynamics of hierarchy and constrained by formality and lack of trust, they speak their lines woodenly and without conviction. Lacking emotional commitment, the people who must carry out the plan don't act decisively.

These faulty interactions rarely occur in isolation. Far more often, they're typical of the way large and small decisions are made—or not made—throughout a company. The inability to take decisive action is rooted in the corporate culture and seems to employees to be impervious to change.

The key word here is "seems," because, in fact, leaders create a culture of indecisiveness, and leaders can break it. The primary instrument at their disposal is the human interactions—the dialogues—through which assumptions are challenged or go unchallenged, information is shared or not shared, disagreements are brought to the surface or papered over. Dialogue is the basic unit of work in an organization. The quality of the dialogue determines how people gather and process information, how they make decisions, and how they feel about one another and about the outcome of these decisions. Dialogue can lead to new ideas and speed as a competitive advantage. It is the single-most important factor underlying the productivity and growth of the knowledge worker. Indeed, the tone and content of dialogue shapes people's behaviors

Idea in Brief

The single greatest cause of corporate underperformance is the failure to execute. According to author Ram Charan, such failures usually result from misfires in personal interactions. And these faulty interactions rarely occur in isolation, Charan says in this article originally published in 2001. More often than not, they're typical of the way large and small decisions are made (or not made) throughout an organization. The inability to take decisive action is rooted in a company's culture. Leaders create this culture of indecisiveness, Charan says—and they can break it by doing three things: First, they must engender intellectual honesty in the connections between people.

Second, they must see to it that the organization's social operating mechanisms—the meetings, reviews, and other situations through which people in the corporation transact business—have honest dialogue at their cores. And third, leaders must ensure that feedback and follow-through are used to reward high achievers, coach those who are struggling, and discourage those whose behaviors are blocking the organization's progress. By taking these three approaches and using every encounter as an opportunity to model open and honest dialogue, leaders can set the tone for an organization, moving it from paralysis to action.

and beliefs—that is, the corporate culture—faster and more permanently than any reward system, structural change, or vision statement I've seen.

Breaking a culture of indecision requires a leader who can engender intellectual honesty and trust in the connections between people. By using each encounter with his or her employees as an opportunity to model open, honest, and decisive dialogue, the leader sets the tone for the entire organization.

But setting the tone is only the first step. To transform a culture of indecision, leaders must also see to it that the organization's *social operating mechanisms*—that is, the executive committee meetings, budget and strategy reviews, and other situations through which the people of a corporation do business—have honest dialogue at their center. These mechanisms set the stage. Tightly linked and consistently practiced, they establish clear lines of accountability for reaching decisions and executing them.

Follow-through and feedback are the final steps in creating a decisive culture. Successful leaders use follow-through and honest feedback to reward high achievers, coach those who are struggling, and redirect the behaviors of those blocking the organization's progress.

In sum, leaders can create a culture of decisive behavior through attention to their own dialogue, the careful design of social operating mechanisms, and appropriate follow-through and feedback.

It All Begins with Dialogue

Studies of successful companies often focus on their products, business models, or operational strengths: Microsoft's world-conquering Windows operating system, Dell's mass customization, Wal-Mart's logistical prowess. Yet products and operational strengths aren't what really set the most successful organizations apart—they can all be rented or imitated. What can't be easily duplicated are the decisive dialogues and robust operating mechanisms and their links to feedback and follow-through. These factors constitute an organization's most enduring competitive advantage, and they are heavily dependent on the character of dialogue that a leader exhibits and thereby influences throughout the organization.

Decisive dialogue is easier to recognize than to define. It encourages incisiveness and creativity and brings coherence to seemingly fragmented and unrelated ideas. It allows tensions to surface and then resolves them by fully airing every relevant viewpoint. Because such dialogue is a process of intellectual inquiry rather than of advocacy, a search for truth rather than a contest, people feel emotionally committed to the outcome. The outcome seems "right" because people have helped shape it. They are energized and ready to act.

Not long ago, I observed the power of a leader's dialogue to shape a company's culture. The setting was the headquarters of a major U.S. multinational. The head of one of the company's largest business units was making a strategy presentation to the CEO and a few of his senior lieutenants. Sounding confident, almost cocky, the unit head laid out his strategy for taking his division from number three in Europe to number one. It was an ambitious plan that hinged on making rapid, sizable market-share gains in Germany, where the company's main competitor was locally based and four times his division's size. The CEO commended his unit head for the inspiring and visionary presentation, then initiated a dialogue to test whether the plan was realistic. "Just how are you going to make these gains?" he wondered aloud. "What other alternatives have you considered? What customers do you plan to acquire?" The unit manager hadn't thought that far ahead. "How have you defined the customers' needs in new and unique ways? How many salespeople do you have?" the CEO asked.

"Ten," answered the unit head.

"How many does your main competitor have?"

"Two hundred," came the sheepish reply.

The boss continued to press: "Who runs Germany for us? Wasn't he in another division up until about three months ago?"

Had the exchange stopped there, the CEO would have only humiliated and discouraged this unit head and sent a message to others in attendance that the risks of thinking big were unacceptably high. But the CEO wasn't interested in killing the strategy and demoralizing the business unit team. Coaching through questioning, he wanted to inject some realism into the dialogue. Speaking bluntly, but not angrily or unkindly, he told the unit manager that he would need more than bravado to take on a formidable German competitor on its home turf. Instead of making a frontal assault, the CEO suggested, why not look for the competition's weak spots and win on speed of execution? Where are the gaps in your competitor's product line? Can you innovate something that can fill those gaps? What customers are the most likely buyers of such a product? Why not zero in on them? Instead of aiming for overall market-share gains, try resegmenting the market. Suddenly, what had appeared to be a dead end opened into new insights, and by the end of the meeting, it was decided that the manager would rethink the strategy and return in 90 days with a more realistic alternative. A key player whose strategy proposal had been flatly rejected left the room feeling energized, challenged, and more sharply focused on the task at hand.

Think about what happened here. Although it might not have been obvious at first, the CEO was not trying to assert his authority or

Dialogue Killers

IS THE DIALOGUE IN YOUR meetings an energy drain? If it doesn't energize people and focus their work, watch for the following.

Dangling Dialogue

Symptom: Confusion prevails. The meeting ends without a clear next step. People create their own self-serving interpretations of the meeting, and no one can be held accountable later when goals aren't met.

Remedy: Give the meeting closure by ensuring that everyone knows who will do what, by when. Do it in writing if necessary, and be specific.

Information Clogs

Symptom: Failure to get all the relevant information into the open. An important fact or opinion comes to light after a decision has been reached, which reopens the decision. This pattern happens repeatedly.

Remedy: Ensure that the right people are in attendance in the first place. When missing information is discovered, disseminate it immediately. Make the expectation for openness and candor explicit by asking, "What's missing?" Use coaching and sanctions to correct information hoarding.

Piecemeal Perspectives

Symptom: People stick to narrow views and self-interests and fail to acknowledge that others have valid interests.

---

diminish the executive. He simply wanted to ensure that the competitive realities were not glossed over and to coach those in attendance on both business acumen and organizational capability as well as on the fine art of asking the right questions. He was challenging the proposed strategy not for personal reasons but for business reasons.

The dialogue affected people's attitudes and behavior in subtle and not so subtle ways: They walked away knowing that they should look for opportunities in unconventional ways and be prepared to answer the inevitable tough questions. They also knew that the CEO was on their side. They became more convinced that growth was possible and that action was necessary. And something else happened: They began to adopt the CEO's tone in subsequent meetings. When, for example, the head of the German unit met with his senior staff to brief them on the new approach to the German market, the questions he fired at his sales chief and product development head

Remedy: Draw people out until you're sure all sides of the issue have been represented. Restate the common purpose repeatedly to keep everyone focused on the big picture. Generate alternatives. Use coaching to show people how their work contributes to the overall mission of the enterprise.

Free-for-All

Symptom: By failing to direct the flow of the discussion, the leader allows negative behaviors to flourish. "Extortionists" hold the whole group for ransom until others see it their way; "sidetrackers" go off on tangents, recount history by saying "When I did this ten years ago . . .," or delve into unnecessary detail; "silent liars" do not express their true opinions, or they agree to things they have no intention of doing; and "dividers" create breaches within the group by seeking support for their viewpoint outside the social operating mechanism or have parallel discussions during the meeting.

Remedy: The leader must exercise inner strength by repeatedly signaling which behaviors are acceptable and by sanctioning those who persist in negative behavior. If less severe sanctions fail, the leader must be willing to remove the offending player from the group.

were pointed, precise, and aimed directly at putting the new strategy into action. He had picked up on his boss's style of relating to others as well as his way of eliciting, sifting, and analyzing information. The entire unit grew more determined and energized.

The chief executive didn't leave the matter there, though. He followed up with a one-page, handwritten letter to the unit head stating the essence of the dialogue and the actions to be executed. And in 90 days, they met again to discuss the revised strategy. (For more on fostering decisive dialogue, see the sidebar "Dialogue Killers.")

How Dialogue Becomes Action

The setting in which dialogue occurs is as important as the dialogue itself. The social operating mechanisms of decisive corporate cultures feature behaviors marked by four characteristics: openness, candor, informality, and closure. Openness means that the outcome is not predetermined. There's an honest search for alternatives and new discoveries. Questions like "What are we missing?" draw people in and signal the leader's willingness to hear all sides. Leaders create an atmosphere of safety that permits spirited discussion, group learning, and trust.

Candor is slightly different. It's a willingness to speak the unspeakable, to expose unfulfilled commitments, to air the conflicts that undermine apparent consensus. Candor means that people express their real opinions, not what they think team players are supposed to say. Candor helps wipe out the silent lies and pocket vetoes that occur when people agree to things they have no intention of acting on. It prevents the kind of unnecessary rework and revisiting of decisions that saps productivity.

Formality suppresses candor; informality encourages it. When presentations and comments are stiff and prepackaged, they signal that the whole meeting has been carefully scripted and orchestrated. Informality has the opposite effect. It reduces defensiveness. People feel more comfortable asking questions and reacting honestly, and the spontaneity is energizing.

If informality loosens the atmosphere, closure imposes discipline. Closure means that at the end of the meeting, people know exactly what they are expected to do. Closure produces decisiveness by assigning accountability and deadlines to people in an open forum. It tests a leader's inner strength and intellectual resources. Lack of closure, coupled with a lack of sanctions, is the primary reason for a culture of indecision.

A robust social operating mechanism consistently includes these four characteristics. Such a mechanism has the right people participating in it, and it occurs with the right frequency.

When Dick Brown arrived at Electronic Data Systems (EDS) in early 1999, he resolved to create a culture that did more than pay lip service to the ideals of collaboration, openness, and decisiveness. He had a big job ahead of him. EDS was known for its bright, aggressive people, but employees had a reputation for competing against one another at least as often as they pulled together. The organization was marked by a culture of lone heroes. Individual operating units had little or no incentive for sharing information or cooperating with one another to win business. There were few sanctions for "lone" behaviors and for failure to meet performance goals. And indecision was rife. As one company veteran puts it, "Meetings, meetings, and more meetings. People couldn't make decisions, wouldn't make decisions. They didn't have to. No accountability." EDS was losing business. Revenue was flat, earnings were on the decline, and the price of the company's stock was down sharply.

A central tenet of Brown's management philosophy is that "leaders get the behavior they tolerate." Shortly after he arrived at EDS, he installed six social operating mechanisms within one year that signaled he would not put up with the old culture of rampant individualism and information hoarding. One mechanism was the "performance call," as it is known around the company. Once a month, the top 100 or so EDS executives worldwide take part in a conference call where the past month's numbers and critical activities are reviewed in detail. Transparency and simultaneous information are the rules; information hoarding is no longer possible. Everyone knows who is on target for the year, who is ahead of projections, and who is behind. Those who are behind must explain the shortfall—and how they plan to get back on track. It's not enough for a manager to say she's assessing, reviewing, or analyzing a problem. Those aren't the words of someone who is acting, Brown says. Those are the words of someone getting ready to act. To use them in front of Brown is to invite two questions in response: When you've finished your analysis, what are you going to do? And how soon are you going to do it? The only way that Brown's people can answer those questions satisfactorily is to make a decision and execute it.

The performance calls are also a mechanism for airing and resolving the conflicts inevitable in a large organization, particularly when it comes to cross selling in order to accelerate revenue growth. Two units may be pursuing the same customer, for example, or a customer serviced by one unit may be acquired by a customer serviced by another. Which unit should lead the pursuit? Which unit should

GE's Secret Weapon

KNOWN FOR ITS STATE-OF-THE-ART management practices, General Electric has forged a system of ten tightly linked social operating mechanisms. Vital to GE's success, these mechanisms set goals and priorities for the whole company as well as for its individual business units and track each unit's progress toward those goals. CEO Jack Welch also uses the system to evaluate senior managers within each unit and reward or sanction them according to their performance.

Three of the most widely imitated of these mechanisms are the Corporate Executive Council (CEC), which meets four times a year; the annual leadership and organizational reviews, known as Session C; and the annual strategy reviews, known as S-1 and S-2. Most large organizations have similar mechanisms. GE's, however, are notable for their intensity and duration; tight links to one another; follow-through; and uninhibited candor, closure, and decisiveness.

At the CEC, the company's senior leaders gather for two-and-a-half days of intensive collaboration and information exchange. As these leaders share best practices, assess the external business environment, and identify the company's most promising opportunities and most pressing problems, Welch has a chance to coach managers and observe their styles of working, thinking, and collaborating. Among the ten initiatives to emerge from these meetings in the past 14 years are GE's Six Sigma quality-improvement drive and its companywide e-commerce effort. These sessions aren't for the faint-hearted—at times, the debates can resemble verbal combat. But by the time the CEC breaks up, everyone in attendance knows both what the corporate priorities are and what's expected of him or her.

At Session C meetings, Welch and GE's senior vice president for human resources, Bill Conaty, meet with the head of each business unit as well as his or her top HR executive to discuss leadership and organizational issues. In these intense 12- to 14-hour sessions, the attendees review the unit's prospective talent pool and its organizational priorities. Who needs to be promoted,

service the merged entity? It's vitally important to resolve these questions. Letting them fester doesn't just drain emotional energy, it shrinks the organization's capacity to act decisively. Lack of speed becomes a competitive disadvantage.

Brown encourages people to bring these conflicts to the surface, both because he views them as a sign of organizational health and because they provide an opportunity to demonstrate the style of rewarded, and developed? How? Who isn't making the grade? Candor is mandatory, and so is execution. The dialogue goes back and forth and links with the strategy of the business unit. Welch follows up each session with a handwritten note reviewing the substance of the dialogue and action items. Through this mechanism, picking and evaluating people has become a core competence at GE. No wonder GE is known as "CEO University."

The unit head's progress in implementing that action plan is among the items on the agenda at the S-1 meeting, held about two months after Session C. Welch, his chief financial officer, and members of the office of the CEO meet individually with each unit head and his or her team to discuss strategy for the next three years. The strategy, which must incorporate the companywide themes and initiatives that emerged from the CEC meetings, is subjected to intensive scrutiny and reality testing by Welch and the senior staff. The dialogue in the sessions is informal, open, decisive, and full of valuable coaching from Welch on both business and human resources issues. As in Session C, the dialogue about strategy links with people and organizational issues. Again, Welch follows up with a handwritten note in which he sets out what he expects of the unit head as a result of the dialogue.

S-2 meetings, normally held in November, follow a similar agenda to the S-1 meeting, except that they are focused on a shorter time horizon, usually 12 to 15 months. Here, operational priorities and resource allocations are linked.

Taken together, the meetings link feedback, decision making, and assessment of the organization's capabilities and key people. The mechanism explicitly ties the goals and performance of each unit to the overall strategy of the corporation and places a premium on the development of the next generation of leaders. The process is unrelenting in its demand for managerial accountability. At the same time, Welch takes the opportunity to engage in follow-through and feedback that is candid, on point, and focused on decisiveness and execution. This operating system may be GE's most enduring competitive advantage.

dialogue he advocates. He tries to create a safe environment for disagreement by reminding employees that the conflict isn't personal.

Conflict in any global organization is built in. And, Brown believes, it's essential if everyone is going to think in terms of the entire organization, not just one little corner of it. Instead of seeking the solution favorable to their unit, they'll look for the solution that's best for EDS and its shareholders. It sounds simple, even obvious. But in an organization once characterized by lone heroes and self-interest, highly visible exercises in conflict resolution remind people to align their interests with the company as a whole. It's not enough to state the message once and assume it will sink in. Behavior is changed through repetition. Stressing the message over and over in social operating mechanisms like the monthly performance calls—and rewarding or sanctioning people based on their adherence to it—is one of Brown's most powerful tools for producing the behavioral changes that usher in genuine cultural change.

Of course, no leader can or should attend every meeting, resolve every conflict, or make every decision. But by designing social operating mechanisms that promote free-flowing yet productive dialogue, leaders strongly influence how others perform these tasks. Indeed, it is through these mechanisms that the work of shaping a decisive culture gets done.

Another corporation that employs social operating mechanisms to create a decisive culture is multinational pharmaceutical giant Pharmacia. The company's approach illustrates a point I stress repeatedly to my clients: Structure divides; social operating mechanisms integrate. I hasten to add that structure is essential. If an organization didn't divide tasks, functions, and responsibilities, it would never get anything done. But social operating mechanisms are required to direct the various activities contained within a structure toward an objective. Well-designed mechanisms perform this integrating function. But no matter how well designed, the mechanisms also need decisive dialogue to work properly.

Two years after its 1995 merger with Upjohn, Pharmacia's CEO Fred Hassan set out to create an entirely new culture for the combined entity. The organization he envisioned would be collaborative, customer focused, and speedy. It would meld the disparate talents of a global enterprise to develop market-leading drugs—and do so faster than the competition. The primary mechanism for fostering collaboration: Leaders from several units and functions would engage in frequent, constructive dialogue.

The company's race to develop a new generation of antibiotics to treat drug-resistant infections afforded Pharmacia's management an opportunity to test the success of its culture-building efforts. Dr. Göran Ando, the chief of research and development, and Carrie Cox, the head of global business management, jointly created a social operating mechanism comprising some of the company's leading scientists, clinicians, and marketers. Just getting the three functions together regularly was a bold step. Typically, drug development proceeds by a series of handoffs. One group of scientists does the basic work of drug discovery, then hands off its results to a second group, which steers the drug through a year or more of clinical trials. If and when it receives the Food and Drug Administration's stamp of approval, it's handed off to the marketing people, who devise a marketing plan. Only then is the drug handed off to the sales department, which pitches it to doctors and hospitals. By supplanting this daisy-chain approach with one that made scientists, clinicians, and marketers jointly responsible for the entire flow of development and marketing, the two leaders aimed to develop a drug that better met the needs of patients, had higher revenue potential, and gained speed as a competitive advantage. And they wanted to create a template for future collaborative efforts.

The company's reward system reinforced this collaborative model by explicitly linking compensation to the actions of the group. Every member's compensation would be based on the time to bring the drug to market, the time for the drug to reach peak profitable share, and total sales. The system gave group members a strong incentive to talk openly with one another and to share information freely. But the creative spark was missing. The first few times the drug development group met, it focused almost exclusively on their differences, which were considerable. Without trafficking in clichés, it is safe to say that scientists, clinicians, and marketers tend to have different ways of speaking, thinking, and relating. And each tended to defend what it viewed as its interests rather than the interests of shareholders and customers. It was at this point that Ando and Cox took charge of the dialogue, reminding the group that it was important to play well with others but even more important to produce a drug that met patients' needs and to beat the competition.

Acting together, the two leaders channeled conversation into productive dialogue focused on a common task. They shared what they knew about developing and marketing pharmaceuticals and demonstrated how scientists could learn to think a little like marketers, and marketers a little like scientists. They tackled the emotional challenge of resolving conflicts in the open in order to demonstrate how to disagree, sometimes strongly, without animosity and without losing sight of their common purpose.

Indeed, consider how one dialogue helped the group make a decision that turned a promising drug into a success story. To simplify the research and testing process, the group's scientists had begun to search for an antibiotic that would be effective against a limited number of infections and would be used only as "salvage therapy" in acute cases, when conventional antibiotic therapies had failed. But intensive dialogue with the marketers yielded the information that doctors were receptive to a drug that would work against a wide spectrum of infections. They wanted a drug that could treat acute infections completely by starting treatment earlier in the course of the disease, either in large doses through an intravenous drip or in smaller doses with a pill. The scientists shifted their focus, and the result was Zyvox, one of the major pharmaceutical success stories of recent years. It has become the poster drug in Pharmacia's campaign for a culture characterized by cross-functional collaboration and speedy execution. Through dialogue, the group created a product that neither the scientists, clinicians, nor marketers acting by themselves could have envisioned or executed. And the mechanism that created this open dialogue is now standard practice at Pharmacia.

Follow-Through and Feedback

Follow-through is in the DNA of decisive cultures and takes place either in person, on the telephone, or in the routine conduct of a social operating mechanism. Lack of follow-through destroys the discipline of execution and encourages indecision.

A culture of indecision changes when groups of people are compelled to always be direct. And few mechanisms encourage directness more effectively than performance and compensation reviews, especially if they are explicitly linked to social operating mechanisms. Yet all too often, the performance review process is as ritualized and empty as the business meeting I described at the beginning of this article. Both the employee and his manager want to get the thing over with as quickly as possible. Check the appropriate box, keep up the good work, here's your raise, and let's be sure to do this again next year. Sorry—gotta run. There's no genuine conversation, no feedback, and worst of all, no chance for the employee to learn the sometimes painful truths that will help her grow and develop. Great compensation systems die for lack of candid dialogue and leaders' emotional fortitude.

At EDS, Dick Brown has devised an evaluation and review process that virtually forces managers to engage in candid dialogue with their subordinates. Everyone at the company is ranked in quintiles and rewarded according to how well they perform compared with their peers. It has proved to be one of the most controversial features of Dick Brown's leadership—some employees view it as a Darwinian means of dividing winners from losers and pitting colleagues against one another.

That isn't the objective of the ranking system, Brown insists. He views the ranking process as the most effective way to reward the company's best performers and show laggards where they need to improve. But the system needs the right sort of dialogue to make it work as intended and serve its purpose of growing the talent pool. Leaders must give honest feedback to their direct reports, especially to those who find themselves at the bottom of the rankings.

Brown recalls one encounter he had shortly after the first set of rankings was issued. An employee who had considered himself one of EDS's best performers was shocked to find himself closer to the bottom of the roster than the top. "How could this be?" the employee asked. "I performed as well this year as I did last year, and last year my boss gave me a stellar review." Brown replied that he could think of two possible explanations. The first was that the employee wasn't as good at his job as he thought he was. The second possibility was that even if the employee was doing as good a job as he did the previous year, his peers were doing better. "If you're staying the same," Brown concluded, "you're falling behind."

That exchange revealed the possibility—the likelihood, even— that the employee's immediate superior had given him a less-than-honest review the year before rather than tackle the unpleasant task of telling him where he was coming up short. Brown understands why a manager might be tempted to duck such a painful conversation. Delivering negative feedback tests the strength of a leader. But critical feedback is part of what Brown calls "the heavy lifting of leadership." Avoiding it, he says, "sentences the organization to mediocrity." What's more, by failing to provide honest feedback, leaders cheat their people by depriving them of the information they need to improve.

Feedback should be many things—candid; constructive; relentlessly focused on behavioral performance, accountability, and execution. One thing it shouldn't be is surprising. "A leader should be constructing his appraisal all year long," Brown says, "and giving his appraisal all year long. You have 20, 30, 60 opportunities a year to share your observations. Don't let those opportunities pass. If, at the end of the year, someone is truly surprised by what you have to say, that's a failure of leadership."

Ultimately, changing a culture of indecision is a matter of leadership. It's a matter of asking hard questions: How robust and effective are our social operating mechanisms? How well are they linked? Do they have the right people and the right frequency? Do they have a rhythm and operate consistently? Is follow-through built in? Are rewards and sanctions linked to the outcomes of the decisive dialogue? Most important, how productive is the dialogue within these mechanisms? Is our dialogue marked by openness, candor, informality, and closure?

Transforming a culture of indecision is an enormous and demanding task. It takes all the listening skills, business acumen, and operational experience that a corporate leader can summon. But just as important, the job demands emotional fortitude, follow-through, and inner strength. Asking the right questions; identifying and resolving conflicts; providing candid, constructive feedback; and differentiating people with sanctions and rewards is never easy. Frequently, it's downright unpleasant. No wonder many senior executives avoid the task. In the short term, they spare themselves considerable emotional wear and tear. But their evasion sets the tone for an organization that can't share intelligence, make decisions, or face conflicts, much less resolve them. Those who evade miss the very point of effective leadership. Leaders with the strength to insist on honest dialogue and follow-through will be rewarded not only with a decisive organization but also with a workforce that is energized, empowered, and engaged.

Originally published in April 2001. Reprint R0601J

What You Don't Know About Making Decisions

by David A. Garvin and Michael A. Roberto

LEADERS SHOW THEIR METTLE IN many ways—setting strategy and motivating people, just to mention two—but above all else leaders are made or broken by the quality of their decisions. That's a given, right? If you answered yes, then you would probably be surprised by how many executives approach decision making in a way that neither puts enough options on the table nor permits sufficient evaluation to ensure that they can make the best choice. Indeed, our research over the past several years strongly suggests that, simply put, most leaders get decision making all wrong.

The reason: Most businesspeople treat decision making as an event—a discrete choice that takes place at a single point in time, whether they're sitting at a desk, moderating a meeting, or staring at a spreadsheet. This classic view of decision making has a pronouncement popping out of a leader's head, based on experience, gut, research, or all three. Say the matter at hand is whether to pull a product with weak sales off the market. An "event" leader would mull in solitude, ask for advice, read reports, mull some more, then say yea or nay and send the organization off to make it happen. But to look at decision making that way is to overlook larger social and organizational contexts, which ultimately determine the success of any decision.

The fact is, decision making is not an event. It's a process, one that unfolds over weeks, months, or even years; one that's fraught with power plays and politics and is replete with personal nuances and institutional history; one that's rife with discussion and debate; and one that requires support at all levels of the organization when it comes time for execution. Our research shows that the difference between leaders who make good decisions and those who make bad ones is striking. The former recognize that all decisions are processes, and they explicitly design and manage them as such. The latter persevere in the fantasy that decisions are events they alone control.

In the following pages, we'll explore how leaders can design and manage a sound, effective decision-making process—an approach we call inquiry—and outline a set of criteria for assessing the quality of the decision-making process. First, a look at the process itself.

Decisions as Process: Inquiry Versus Advocacy

Not all decision-making processes are equally effective, particularly in the degree to which they allow a group to identify and consider a wide range of ideas. In our research, we've seen two broad approaches. *Inquiry*, which we prefer, is a very open process designed to generate multiple alternatives, foster the exchange of ideas, and produce a well-tested solution. Unfortunately, this approach doesn't come easily or naturally to most people. Instead, groups charged with making a decision tend to default to the second mode, one we call *advocacy*. The two look deceptively similar on the surface: groups of people, immersed in discussion and debate, trying to select a course of action by drawing on what they believe is the best available evidence. But despite their similarities, inquiry and advocacy produce dramatically different results.

When a group takes an advocacy perspective, participants approach decision making as a contest, although they don't necessarily compete openly or even consciously. Well-defined groups with special interests—dueling divisions in search of budget increases, for example—advocate for particular positions. Participants are

Idea in Brief

The quality of a leader's decisions can make or break him. Yet most of us get decision making all wrong. Why? We take the least productive approach: **advocacy**. We argue our position with a passion that prevents us from weighing opposing views. We downplay our position's weaknesses to boost our chances of "winning." And we march into decision-making discussions armed for a battle of wills. The consequences? Fractious exchanges that discourage innovative thinking and stifle diverse, valuable viewpoints.

Contrast advocacy with **inquiry**—a much more productive decision-making approach. With inquiry, you carefully consider a variety of options, work with others to discover the best solutions, and stimulate creative thinking rather than suppressing dissension. The payoff? High-quality decisions that advance your company's objectives, and that you reach in a timely manner and implement effectively.

Inquiry isn't easy. You must promote constructive conflict and accept ambiguity. You also must balance *divergence* during early discussions with *unity* during implementation.

How to accomplish this feat? Master the "three C's" of decision making: **conflict, consideration, and closure.**

passionate about their preferred solutions and therefore stand firm in the face of disagreement. That level of passion makes it nearly impossible to remain objective, limiting people's ability to pay attention to opposing arguments. Advocates often present information selectively, buttressing their arguments while withholding relevant conflicting data. Their goal, after all, is to make a compelling case, not to convey an evenhanded or balanced view. Two different plant managers pushing their own improvement programs, for example, may be wary of reporting potential weak points for fear that full disclosure will jeopardize their chances of winning the debate and gaining access to needed resources.

What's more, the disagreements that arise are frequently fractious and even antagonistic. Personalities and egos come into play, and differences are normally resolved through battles of wills and behind-the-scenes maneuvering. The implicit assumption is that a superior solution will emerge from a test of strength among

Idea in Practice

Constructive Conflict

Conflict during decision making takes two forms: *cognitive* (relating to the substance of the work) and *affective* (stemming from interpersonal friction). The first is crucial to effective decision making; the second, destructive. To increase cognitive conflict while decreasing affective:

- **Require vigorous debate.** As a rule, ask tough questions and expect well-framed responses. Pose unexpected theoretical questions that stimulate productive thinking.

- **Prohibit language that triggers defensiveness.** Preface contradictory remarks or questions with phrases that remove blame and fault. ("Your arguments make good sense, but let me play devil's advocate for a moment.")

- **Break up natural coalitions.** Assign people to tasks without consideration of traditional loyalties. Require people with different interests to work together.

- **Shift individuals out of well-worn grooves.** During decision making, ask people to play functional or managerial roles different from their own; for example, lower-level employees assume a CEO's perspective.

- **Challenge stalemated participants to revisit key information.** Ask them to examine underlying assumptions and gather more facts.

Consideration

To gain your team's acceptance and support of a decision-making outcome—even if you've rejected their recommendations—ensure that they perceive the decision-making process as fair. How? Demonstrate consideration throughout the process:

- At the outset, **convey openness** to new ideas and willingness

competing positions. But in fact this approach typically suppresses innovation and encourages participants to go along with the dominant view to avoid further conflict.

By contrast, an inquiry-focused group carefully considers a variety of options and works together to discover the best solution. While people naturally continue to have their own interests, the goal is not to persuade the group to adopt a given point of view but instead to come to agreement on the best course of action. People share information widely, preferably in raw form, to allow participants to draw their own to accept different views. Avoid indicating you've already made up your mind.

- During the discussion, **listen attentively**. Make eye contact and show patience while others explain their positions. Take notes, ask questions, and probe for deeper explanations.

- Afterward, **explain the rationale behind your decision**. Detail the criteria you used to select a course of action. Spell out how each participant's arguments affected the final decision.

Closure

In addition to stimulating constructive conflict and showing consideration, bring the decision process to closure at the appropriate time. Watch for two problems:

- **Deciding too early.** Worried about being dissenters, decision participants may readily accept the first plausible option rather

than thoughtfully analyzing options. Unstated objections surface later—preventing cooperative action during the crucial implementation stage.

Watch for latent discontent in body language—furrowed brows, crossed arms, the curled-up posture of defiance. Call for a break, encourage each dissenter to speak up, then reconvene. Seek input from people known for raising hard questions and offering fresh perspectives.

- **Deciding too late.** Warring factions face off, restating their positions repeatedly. Or, striving for fairness, people insist on hearing every view and resolving every question before reaching closure.

To escape these endless loops, announce a decision. Accept that the decision-making process is ambiguous and that you'll never have complete, unequivocal data.

conclusions. Rather than suppressing dissension, an inquiry process encourages critical thinking. All participants feel comfortable raising alternative solutions and asking hard questions about the possibilities already on the table.

People engaged in an inquiry process rigorously question proposals and the assumptions they rest on, so conflict may be intense—but it is seldom personal. In fact, because disagreements revolve around ideas and interpretations rather than entrenched positions, conflict is generally healthy, and team members resolve their differ-

Two approaches to decision making

	Advocacy	Inquiry
Concept of decision making	a contest	collaborative problem solving
Purpose of discussion	persuasion and lobbying	testing and evaluation
Participants' role	spokespeople	critical thinkers
Patterns of behavior	strive to persuade others defend your position downplay weaknesses	present balanced arguments remain open to alternatives accept constructive criticism
Minority views	discouraged or dismissed	cultivated and valued
Outcome	winners and losers	collective ownership

ences by applying rules of reason. The implicit assumption is that a consummate solution will emerge from a test of strength among competing ideas rather than dueling positions. Recent accounts of GE's succession process describe board members pursuing just such an open-minded approach. All members met repeatedly with the major candidates and gathered regularly to review their strengths and weaknesses—frequently without Jack Welch in attendance—with little or no attempt to lobby early for a particular choice.

A process characterized by inquiry rather than advocacy tends to produce decisions of higher quality—decisions that not only advance the company's objectives but also are reached in a timely manner and can be implemented effectively. Therefore, we believe that leaders seeking to improve their organizations' decision-making capabilities need to begin with a single goal: moving as quickly as possible from a process of advocacy to one of inquiry.

That requires careful attention to three critical factors, the "three C's" of effective decision making: *conflict, consideration,* and *closure.* Each entails a delicate balancing act.

Constructive Conflict

Critical thinking and rigorous debate invariably lead to conflict. The good news is that conflict brings issues into focus, allowing leaders to make more informed choices. The bad news is that the wrong kind of conflict can derail the decision-making process altogether.

Indeed, conflict comes in two forms—*cognitive* and *affective.* Cognitive, or substantive, conflict relates to the work at hand. It involves disagreements over ideas and assumptions and differing views on the best way to proceed. Not only is such conflict healthy, it's crucial to effective inquiry. When people express differences openly and challenge underlying assumptions, they can flag real weaknesses and introduce new ideas. Affective, or interpersonal, conflict is emotional. It involves personal friction, rivalries, and clashing personalities, and it tends to diminish people's willingness to cooperate during implementation, rendering the decision-making process less effective. Not surprisingly, it is a common feature of advocacy processes.

On examination, the two are easy to distinguish. When a team member recalls "tough debates about the strategic, financial, and operating merits of the three acquisition candidates," she is referring to cognitive conflict. When a team member comments on "heated arguments that degenerated into personal attacks," he means affective conflict. But in practice the two types of conflict are surprisingly hard to separate. People tend to take any criticism personally and react defensively. The atmosphere quickly becomes charged, and even if a high-quality decision emerges, the emotional fallout tends to linger, making it hard for team members to work together during implementation.

The challenge for leaders is to increase cognitive conflict while keeping affective conflict low—no mean feat. One technique is to establish norms that make vigorous debate the rule rather than the exception. Chuck Knight, for 27 years the CEO of Emerson Electric, accomplished this by relentlessly grilling managers during planning reviews, no matter what he actually thought of the proposal on the table, asking tough, combative questions and expecting well-framed responses. The process—which Knight called the "logic of illogic" because of his willingness to test even well-crafted arguments by raising unexpected, and occasionally fanciful, concerns—was undoubtedly intimidating. But during his tenure it produced a steady stream of smart investment decisions and an unbroken string of quarterly increases in net income.

Bob Galvin, when he was CEO of Motorola in the 1980s, took a slightly different approach. He habitually asked unexpected hypothetical questions that stimulated creative thinking. Subsequently, as chairman of the board of overseers for the Malcolm Baldrige National Quality Program, Galvin took his colleagues by surprise when, in response to pressure from constituents to broaden the criteria for the award, he proposed narrowing them instead. In the end, the board did in fact broaden the criteria, but his seemingly out-of-the-blue suggestion sparked a creative and highly productive debate.

Another technique is to structure the conversation so that the process, by its very nature, fosters debate. This can be done by dividing people into groups with different, and often competing, responsibilities. For example, one group may be asked to develop a proposal while the other generates alternative recommendations. Then the groups would exchange proposals and discuss the various options. Such techniques virtually guarantee high levels of cognitive conflict. (The exhibit "Structuring the debate" outlines two approaches for using different groups to stimulate creative thinking.)

But even if you've structured the process with an eye toward encouraging cognitive conflict, there's always a risk that it will become personal. Beyond cooling the debate with "time-outs," skilled leaders use a number of creative techniques to elevate cognitive debate while minimizing affective conflict.

Structuring the debate

By breaking a decision-making body into two subgroups, leaders can often create an environment in which people feel more comfortable engaging in debate. Scholars recommend two techniques in particular, which we call the "point-counterpoint" and "intellectual watchdog" approaches. The first three steps are the same for both techniques:

Point-counterpoint	Intellectual watchdog
The team divides into two subgroups.	The team divides into two subgroups.
Subgroup A develops a proposal, fleshing out the recommendation, the key assumptions, and the critical supporting data.	Subgroup A develops a proposal, fleshing out the recommendation, the key assumptions, and the critical supporting data.
Subgroup A presents the proposal to Subgroup B in written and oral forms.	Subgroup A presents the proposal to Subgroup B in written and oral forms.
Subgroup B generates one or more alternative plans of action.	Subgroup B develops a detailed critique of these assumptions and recommendations. It presents this critique in written and oral forms. Subgroup A revises its proposal based on this feedback.
The subgroups come together to debate the proposals and seek agreement on a common set of assumptions.	The subgroups continue in this revision-critique-revision cycle until they converge on a common set of assumptions.
Based on those assumptions, the subgroups continue to debate various options and strive to agree on a common set of recommendations.	Then, the subgroups work together to develop a common set of recommendations.

First, adroit leaders pay careful attention to the way issues are framed, as well as to the language used during discussions. They preface contradictory remarks or questions with phrases that remove some of the personal sting ("Your arguments make good sense, but let me play devil's advocate for a moment"). They also set ground rules about language, insisting that team members avoid words and behavior that trigger defensiveness. For instance, in the U.S. Army's after-action reviews, conducted immediately after missions to identify mistakes so they can be avoided next time, facilitators make a point of saying, "We don't use the 'b' word, and we don't use the 'f' word. We don't place blame, and we don't find fault."

Second, leaders can help people step back from their preestablished positions by breaking up natural coalitions and assigning people to tasks on some basis other than traditional loyalties. At a leading aerospace company, one business unit president had to deal with two powerful coalitions within his organization during a critical decision about entering into a strategic alliance. When he set up two groups to consider alternative alliance partners, he interspersed the groups with members of each coalition, forcing people with different interests to work with one another. He then asked both groups to evaluate the same wide range of options using different criteria (such as technological capability, manufacturing prowess, or project management skills). The two groups then shared their evaluations and worked together to select the best partner. Because nobody had complete information, they were forced to listen closely to one another.

Third, leaders can shift individuals out of well-grooved patterns, where vested interests are highest. They can, for example, ask team members to research and argue for a position they did not endorse during initial discussions. Similarly, they can assign team members to play functional or managerial roles different from their own, such as asking an operations executive to take the marketing view or asking a lower-level employee to assume the CEO's strategic perspective.

Finally, leaders can ask participants locked in debate to revisit key facts and assumptions and gather more information. Often, people become so focused on the differences between opposing positions that they reach a stalemate. Emotional conflict soon follows. Asking people to examine underlying presumptions can defuse the tension and set the team back on track. For instance, at Enron, when people disagree strongly about whether or not to apply their trading skills to a new commodity or market, senior executives quickly refocus the discussion on characteristics of industry structure and assumptions about market size and customer preferences. People quickly recognize areas of agreement, discover precisely how and why they disagree, and then focus their debate on specific issues.

Consideration

Once a decision's been made and the alternatives dismissed, some people will have to surrender the solution they preferred. At times, those who are overruled resist the outcome; at other times, they display grudging acceptance. What accounts for the difference? The critical factor appears to be the perception of fairness—what scholars call "procedural justice." The reality is that the leader will make the ultimate decision, but the people participating in the process must believe that their views were considered and that they had a genuine opportunity to influence the final decision. Researchers have found that if participants believe the process was fair, they are far more willing to commit themselves to the resulting decision even if their views did not prevail. (For a detailed discussion of this phenomenon, see W. Chan Kim and Renée Mauborgne, "Fair Process: Managing in the Knowledge Economy," HBR July–August 1997).

Many managers equate fairness with *voice*—with giving everyone a chance to express his or her own views. They doggedly work their way around the table, getting everyone's input. However, voice is not nearly as important as *consideration*—people's belief that the leader actively listened to them during the discussions and weighed their views carefully before reaching a decision. In his 1999 book, *Only the Paranoid Survive*, Intel's chairman Andy Grove describes how he explains the distinction to his middle managers: "Your criterion for involvement should be that you're heard and understood. . . . All sides cannot prevail in the debate, but all opinions have value in shaping the right answer."

In fact, voice without consideration is often damaging; it leads to resentment and frustration rather than to acceptance. When the time comes to implement the decision, people are likely to drag their feet if

Advocacy Versus Inquiry in Action: The Bay of Pigs and the Cuban Missile Crisis

PERHAPS THE BEST DEMONSTRATION OF advocacy versus inquiry comes from the administration of President John F. Kennedy. During his first two years in office, Kennedy wrestled with two critical foreign policy decisions: the Bay of Pigs invasion and the Cuban Missile Crisis. Both were assigned to cabinet-level task forces, involving many of the same players, the same political interests, and extremely high stakes. But the results were extraordinarily different, largely because the two groups operated in different modes.

The first group, charged with deciding whether to support an invasion of Cuba by a small army of U.S.-trained Cuban exiles, worked in advocacy mode, and the outcome is widely regarded as an example of flawed decision making. Shortly after taking office, President Kennedy learned of the planned attack on Cuba developed by the CIA during the Eisenhower administration. Backed by the Joint Chiefs of Staff, the CIA argued forcefully for the invasion and minimized the risks, filtering the information presented to the president to reinforce the agency's position. Knowledgeable individuals on the State Department's Latin America desk were excluded from deliberations because of their likely opposition.

Some members of Kennedy's staff opposed the plan but held their tongues for fear of appearing weak in the face of strong advocacy by the CIA. As a result, there was little debate, and the group failed to test some critical underlying assumptions. For example, they didn't question whether the landing would in fact lead to a rapid domestic uprising against Castro, and they failed to find out whether the exiles could fade into the mountains (which were 80 miles from the landing site) should they meet with strong resistance. The resulting invasion is generally considered to be one of the low points of the Cold War. About 100 lives were lost, and the rest of the exiles were taken hostage. The incident was a major embarrassment to the Kennedy administration and dealt a blow to America's global standing.

After the botched invasion, Kennedy conducted a review of the foreign policy decision-making process and introduced five major changes, essentially transforming the process into one of inquiry. First, people were urged to participate in discussions as "skeptical generalists"—that is, as disinterested

they sense that the decision-making process had been a sham—an exercise in going through the motions designed to validate the leader's preferred solution. This appears to have been true of the Daimler-Chrysler merger. Daimler CEO Jurgen Schrempp asked for critical thinkers rather than as representatives of particular departments. Second, Robert Kennedy and Theodore Sorensen were assigned the role of intellectual watchdog, expected to pursue every possible point of contention, uncovering weaknesses and untested assumptions. Third, task forces were urged to abandon the rules of protocol, eliminating formal agendas and deference to rank. Fourth, participants were expected to split occasionally into subgroups to develop a broad range of options. And finally, President Kennedy decided to absent himself from some of the early task force meetings to avoid influencing other participants and slanting the debate.

The inquiry mode was used to great effect when in October 1962 President Kennedy learned that the Soviet Union had placed nuclear missiles on Cuban soil, despite repeated assurances from the Soviet ambassador that this would not occur. Kennedy immediately convened a high-level task force, which contained many of the same men responsible for the Bay of Pigs invasion, and asked them to frame a response. The group met night and day for two weeks, often inviting additional members to join in their deliberations to broaden their perspective. Occasionally, to encourage the free flow of ideas, they met without the president. Robert Kennedy played his new role thoughtfully, critiquing options frequently and encouraging the group to develop additional alternatives. In particular, he urged the group to move beyond a simple go-no-go decision on a military air strike.

Ultimately, subgroups developed two positions, one favoring a blockade and the other an air strike. These groups gathered information from a broad range of sources, viewed and interpreted the same intelligence photos, and took great care to identify and test underlying assumptions, such as whether the Tactical Air Command was indeed capable of eliminating all Soviet missiles in a surgical air strike. The subgroups exchanged position papers, critiqued each other's proposals, and came together to debate the alternatives. They presented Kennedy with both options, leaving him to make the final choice. The result was a carefully framed response, leading to a successful blockade and a peaceful end to the crisis.

extensive analysis and assessment of potential merger candidates but had long before settled on Chrysler as his choice. In fact, when consultants told him that his strategy was unlikely to create shareholder value, he dismissed the data and went ahead with his plans.

Schrempp may have solicited views from many parties, but he clearly failed to give them much weight.

Leaders can demonstrate consideration throughout the decision-making process. At the outset, they need to convey openness to new ideas and a willingness to accept views that differ from their own. In particular, they must avoid suggesting that their minds are already made up. They should avoid disclosing their personal preferences early in the process, or they should clearly state that any initial opinions are provisional and subject to change. Or they can absent themselves from early deliberations.

During the discussions, leaders must take care to show that they are listening actively and attentively. How? By asking questions, probing for deeper explanations, echoing comments, making eye contact, and showing patience when participants explain their positions. Taking notes is an especially powerful signal, since it suggests that the leader is making a real effort to capture, understand, and evaluate people's thoughts.

And after they make the final choice, leaders should explain their logic. They must describe the rationale for their decision, detailing the criteria they used to select a course of action. Perhaps more important, they need to convey how each participant's arguments affected the final decision or explain clearly why they chose to differ with those views.

Closure

Knowing when to end deliberations is tricky; all too often decision-making bodies rush to a conclusion or else dither endlessly and decide too late. Deciding too early is as damaging as deciding too late, and both problems can usually be traced to unchecked advocacy.

Deciding too early
Sometimes people's desire to be considered team players overrides their willingness to engage in critical thinking and thoughtful analysis, so the group readily accepts the first remotely plausible option. Popularly known as "groupthink," this mind-set is prevalent in the

presence of strong advocates, especially in new teams, whose members are still learning the rules and may be less willing to stand out as dissenters.

The danger of groupthink is not only that it suppresses the full range of options but also that unstated objections will come to the surface at some critical moment—usually at a time when aligned, cooperative action is essential to implementation. The leader of a large division of a fast-growing retailer learned this the hard way. He liked to work with a small subset of his senior team to generate options, evaluate the alternatives, and develop a plan of action, and then bring the proposal back to the full team for validation. At that point, his managers would feel they had been presented with a fait accompli and so would be reluctant to raise their concerns. As one of them put it: "Because the meeting is the wrong place to object, we don't walk out of the room as a unified group." Instead, they would reopen the debate during implementation, delaying important initiatives by many months.

As their first line of defense against group-think, leaders need to learn to recognize latent discontent, paying special attention to body language: furrowed brows, crossed arms, or curled-up defiance. To bring disaffected people back into the discussion, it may be best to call for a break, approach dissenters one by one, encourage them to speak up, and then reconvene. GM's Alfred Sloan was famous for this approach, which he would introduce with the following speech: "I take it we are all in complete agreement on the decision here. Then I propose we postpone further discussion of the matter until our next meeting to give ourselves time to develop disagreement and perhaps gain some understanding of what the decision is all about."

Another way to avoid early closure is to cultivate minority views either through norms or through explicit rules. Minority views broaden and deepen debate; they stretch a group's thinking, even though they are seldom adopted intact. It is for this reason that Andy Grove routinely seeks input from "helpful Cassandras," people who are known for raising hard questions and offering fresh perspectives about the dangers of proposed policies.

Deciding too late

Here, too, unchecked advocacy is frequently the source of the problem, and in these instances it takes two main forms. At times, a team hits gridlock: Warring factions refuse to yield, restating their positions over and over again. Without a mechanism for breaking the deadlock, discussions become an endless loop. At other times, people bend over backward to ensure evenhanded participation. Striving for fairness, team members insist on hearing every view and resolving every question before reaching a conclusion. This demand for certainty—for complete arguments backed by unassailable data—is its own peculiar form of advocacy. Once again, the result is usually an endless loop, replaying the same alternatives, objections, and requests for further information. Any member of the group can unilaterally derail the discussion by voicing doubts. Meanwhile, competitive pressures may be demanding an immediate response, or participants may have tuned out long ago, as the same arguments are repeated ad nauseam.

At this point, it's the leader's job to "call the question." Jamie Houghton, the longtime CEO of Corning, invented a vivid metaphor to describe this role. He spoke of wearing two hats when working with his senior team: He figuratively put on his cowboy hat when he wanted to debate with members as an equal, and he donned a bowler when, as CEO, he called the question and announced a decision. The former role allowed for challenges and continued discussion; the latter signaled an end to the debate.

The message here is that leaders—and their teams—need to become more comfortable with ambiguity and be willing to make speedy decisions in the absence of complete, unequivocal data or support. As Dean Stanley Teele of Harvard Business School was fond of telling students: "The art of management is the art of making meaningful generalizations out of inadequate facts."

A Litmus Test

Unfortunately, superior decision making is distressingly difficult to assess in real time. Successful outcomes—decisions of high quality, made in a timely manner and implemented effectively—can be evaluated only after the fact. But by the time the results are in, it's normally too late to take corrective action. Is there any way to find out earlier whether you're on the right track?

There is indeed. The trick, we believe, is to periodically assess the decision-making process, even as it is under way. Scholars now have considerable evidence showing that a small set of process traits is closely linked with superior outcomes. While they are no guarantee of success, their combined presence sharply improves the odds that you'll make a good decision.

Multiple alternatives

When groups consider many alternatives, they engage in more thoughtful analysis and usually avoid settling too quickly on the easy, obvious answer. This is one reason techniques like point-counterpoint, which requires groups to generate at least two alternatives, are so often associated with superior decision making. Usually, keeping track of the number of options being considered will tell if this test has been met. But take care not to double count. Go-no-go choices involve only one option and don't qualify as two alternatives.

Assumption testing

"Facts" come in two varieties: those that have been carefully tested and those that have been merely asserted or assumed. Effective decision-making groups do not confuse the two. They periodically step back from their arguments and try to confirm their assumptions by examining them critically. If they find that some still lack hard evidence, they may elect to proceed, but they will at least know they're venturing into uncertain territory. Alternatively, the group may designate "intellectual watchdogs" who are assigned the task of scrutinizing the process for unchecked assumptions and challenging them on the spot.

Well-defined criteria

Without crisp, clear goals, it's easy to fall into the trap of comparing apples with oranges. Competing arguments become difficult to judge, since advocates will suggest using those measures (net income, return on capital, market presence, share of mind, and so on) that favor their preferred alternative. Fuzzy thinking and long delays are the likely result.

To avoid the problem, the team should specify goals up front and revisit them repeatedly during the decision-making process. These goals can be complex and multifaceted, quantitative and qualitative, but whatever form they take, they must remain at the fore. Studies of merger decisions have found that as the process reaches its final stages and managers feel the pressure of deadlines and the rush to close, they often compromise or adjust the criteria they originally created for judging the appropriateness of the deal.

Dissent and debate

David Hume, the great Scottish philosopher, argued persuasively for the merits of debate when he observed that the "truth springs from arguments amongst friends." There are two ways to measure the health of a debate: the kinds of questions being asked and the level of listening.

Some questions open up discussion; others narrow it and end deliberations. Contrarian hypothetical questions usually trigger healthy debate. A manager who worked for former American Express CEO Harvey Golub points to a time when the company was committed to lowering credit card fees, and Golub unexpectedly proposed raising fees instead. "I don't think he meant it seriously," says the manager. "But he certainly taught us how to think about fees."

The level of listening is an equally important indicator of a healthy decision-making process. Poor listening produces flawed analysis as well as personal friction. If participants routinely interrupt one another or pile on rebuttals before digesting the preceding comment, affective conflict is likely to materialize. Civilized discussions quickly become impossible, for collegiality and group harmony usually disappear in the absence of active listening.

Perceived fairness

A real-time measure of perceived fairness is the level of participation that's maintained after a key midpoint or milestone has been reached. Often, a drop in participation is an early warning of problems with implementation since some members of the group are already showing their displeasure by voting with their feet.

In fact, keeping people involved in the process is, in the end, perhaps the most crucial factor in making a decision—and making it stick. It's a job that lies at the heart of leadership and one that uniquely combines the leader's numerous talents. It requires the fortitude to promote conflict while accepting ambiguity, the wisdom to know when to bring conversations to a close, the patience to help others understand the reasoning behind your choice, and, not least, a genius for balance—the ability to embrace both the divergence that may characterize early discussions and the unity needed for effective implementation. Cyrus the Great, the founder of the Persian Empire and a renowned military leader, understood the true hallmark of leadership in the sixth century BC, when he attributed his success to "diversity in counsel, unity in command."

Originally published in August 2001. Reprint R0108G

Who Has the D?

How Clear Decision Roles Enhance
Organizational Performance.
by Paul Rogers and Marcia Blenko

DECISIONS ARE THE COIN OF the realm in business. Every success, every mishap, every opportunity seized or missed is the result of a decision that someone made or failed to make. At many companies, decisions routinely get stuck inside the organization like loose change. But it's more than loose change that's at stake, of course; it's the performance of the entire organization. Never mind what industry you're in, how big and well known your company may be, or how clever your strategy is. If you can't make the right decisions quickly and effectively, and execute those decisions consistently, your business will lose ground.

Indeed, making good decisions and making them happen quickly are the hallmarks of high-performing organizations. When we surveyed executives at 350 global companies about their organizational effectiveness, only 15% said that they have an organization that helps the business outperform competitors. What sets those top performers apart is the quality, speed, and execution of their decision making. The most effective organizations score well on the major strategic decisions—which markets to enter or exit, which businesses to buy or sell, where to allocate capital and talent. But they truly shine when it comes to the critical operating decisions requiring consistency and speed—how to drive product innovation, the best way to position brands, how to manage channel partners.

Even in companies respected for their decisiveness, however, there can be ambiguity over who is accountable for which decisions. As a result, the entire decision-making process can stall, usually at one of four bottlenecks: global versus local, center versus business unit, function versus function, and inside versus outside partners.

The first of these bottlenecks, *global versus local* decision making, can occur in nearly every major business process and function. Decisions about brand building and product development frequently get snared here, when companies wrestle over how much authority local businesses should have to tailor products for their markets. Marketing is another classic global versus local issue—should local markets have the power to determine pricing and advertising?

The second bottleneck, *center versus business unit* decision making, tends to afflict parent companies and their subsidiaries. Business units are on the front line, close to the customer; the center sees the big picture, sets broad goals, and keeps the organization focused on winning. Where should the decision-making power lie? Should a major capital investment, for example, depend on the approval of the business unit that will own it, or should headquarters make the final call?

Function versus function decision making is perhaps the most common bottleneck. Every manufacturer, for instance, faces a balancing act between product development and marketing during the design of a new product. Who should decide what? Cross-functional decisions too often result in ineffective compromise solutions, which frequently need to be revisited because the right people were not involved at the outset.

The fourth decision-making bottleneck, *inside versus outside partners,* has become familiar with the rise of outsourcing, joint ventures, strategic alliances, and franchising. In such arrangements, companies need to be absolutely clear about which decisions can be owned by the external partner (usually those about the execution of strategy) and which must continue to be made internally (decisions about the strategy itself). In the case of outsourcing, for instance, brand-name apparel and footwear marketers once assumed that overseas suppliers could be responsible for decisions about plant employees' wages and working conditions. Big mistake.

Idea in Brief

Decisions are the coin of the realm in business. Every success, every mishap, every opportunity seized or missed stems from a decision someone made—or failed to make. Yet in many firms, decisions routinely stall inside the organization—hurting the entire company's performance.

The culprit? Ambiguity over who's accountable for which decisions. In one auto manufacturer that was missing milestones for rolling out new models, marketers *and* product developers each thought they were responsible for deciding new models' standard features and colors. Result? Conflict over who had final say, endless revisiting of decisions—and missed deadlines that led to lost sales.

How to clarify decision accountability? Assign clear roles for the decisions that most affect your firm's performance—such as which markets to enter, where to allocate capital, and how to drive product innovation. Think "RAPID": Who should recommend a course of action on a key decision? Who must agree to a recommendation before it can move forward? Who will perform the actions needed to implement the decision? Whose input is needed to determine the proposal's feasibility? Who decides—brings the decision to closure and commits the organization to implement it?

When you clarify decision roles, you make the *right* choices—swiftly and effectively.

Clearing the Bottlenecks

The most important step in unclogging decision-making bottlenecks is assigning clear roles and responsibilities. Good decision makers recognize which decisions really matter to performance. They think through who should recommend a particular path, who needs to agree, who should have input, who has ultimate responsibility for making the decision, and who is accountable for follow-through. They make the process routine. The result: better coordination and quicker response times.

Companies have devised a number of methods to clarify decision roles and assign responsibilities. We have used an approach called RAPID, which has evolved over the years, to help hundreds of companies develop clear decision-making guidelines. It is, for sure, not a panacea (an indecisive decision maker, for example, can ruin any good system), but it's an important start. The letters in RAPID stand for the

Idea in Practice

The RAPID Decision Model

For every strategic decision, assign the following roles and responsibilities:

People who . . .	Are responsible for . . .
Recommend	• Making a proposal on a key decision, gathering input, and providing data and analysis to make a sensible choice in a timely fashion • Consulting with input providers—hearing and incorporating their views, and winning their buy-in
Agree	• Negotiating a modified proposal with the recommender if they have concerns about the original proposal • Escalating unresolved issues to the decider if the "A" and "R" can't resolve differences • If necessary, exercising veto power over the recommendation
Perform	• Executing a decision once it's made • Seeing that the decision is implemented promptly and effectively
Input	• Providing relevant facts to the recommender that shed light on the proposal's feasibility and practical implications
Decide	• Serving as the single point of accountability • Bringing the decision to closure by resolving any impasse in the decision-making process • Committing the organization to implementing the decision

primary roles in any decision-making process, although these roles are not performed exactly in this order: recommend, agree, perform, input, and decide—the "D." (See the sidebar "A Decision-Making Primer.")

The people who *recommend* a course of action are responsible for making a proposal or offering alternatives. They need data and analysis to support their recommendations, as well as common sense about what's reasonable, practical, and effective.

The people who *agree* to a recommendation are those who need to sign off on it before it can move forward. If they veto a proposal,

Decision-Role Pitfalls

In assigning decision roles:

- Ensure that only one person "has the D." If two or more people think they're in charge of a particular decision, a tug-of-war results.

- Watch for a proliferation of "A's." Too many people with veto power can paralyze recommenders. If many people must agree, you probably haven't pushed decisions down far enough in your organization.

- Avoid assigning too many "I's." When many people give input, at least some of them aren't making meaningful contributions.

The RAPID Model in Action

Example: At British department-store chain John Lewis, company buyers wanted to increase sales and reduce complexity by offering fewer salt and pepper mill models. The company launched the streamlined product set without involving the sales staff. And sales fell. Upon visiting the stores, buyers saw that salespeople (not understanding the strategy behind the recommendation) had halved shelf space to match the reduction in product range, rather than maintaining the same space but stocking more of the products.

To fix the problem, the company "gave buyers the D" on how much space product categories would have. Sales staff "had the A": If space allocations didn't make sense to them, they could force additional negotiations. They also "had the P," implementing product layouts in stores.

Once decision roles were clarified, sales of salt and pepper mills exceeded original levels.

they must either work with the recommender to come up with an alternative or elevate the issue to the person with the D. For decision making to function smoothly, only a few people should have such veto power. They may be executives responsible for legal or regulatory compliance or the heads of units whose operations will be significantly affected by the decision.

People with *input* responsibilities are consulted about the recommendation. Their role is to provide the relevant facts that are the basis of any good decision: How practical is the proposal? Can manufacturing accommodate the design change? Where there's dissent or

A Decision-Making Primer

GOOD DECISION MAKING DEPENDS ON assigning clear and specific roles. This sounds simple enough, but many companies struggle to make decisions because lots of people feel accountable—or no one does. RAPID and other tools used to analyze decision making give senior management teams a method for assigning roles and involving the relevant people. The key is to be clear who has input, who gets to decide, and who gets it done.

The five letters in RAPID correspond to the five critical decision-making roles: recommend, agree, perform, input, and decide. As you'll see, the roles are not carried out lockstep in this order—we took some liberties for the sake of creating a useful acronym.

Recommend

People in this role are responsible for making a proposal, gathering input, and providing the right data and analysis to make a sensible decision in a timely fashion. In the course of developing a proposal, recommenders consult with the people who provide input, not just hearing and incorporating their views but also building buy in along the way. Recommenders must have analytical skills, common sense, and organizational smarts.

Agree

Individuals in this role have veto power—yes or no—over the recommendation. Exercising the veto triggers a debate between themselves and the recommenders, which should lead to a modified proposal. If that takes too long, or if the two parties simply can't agree, they can escalate the issue to the person who has the D.

Input

These people are consulted on the decision. Because the people who provide input are typically involved in implementation, recommenders have a strong

contrasting views, it's important to get these people to the table at the right time. The recommender has no obligation to act on the input he or she receives but is expected to take it into account—particularly since the people who provide input are generally among those who must implement a decision. Consensus is a worthy goal, but as a decision-making standard, it can be an obstacle to action or a recipe for lowest-common-denominator compromise. A more practical objective is to get everyone involved to buy in to the decision.

interest in taking their advice seriously. No input is binding, but this shouldn't undermine its importance. If the right people are not involved and motivated, the decision is far more likely to falter during execution.

Decide

The person with the D is the formal decision maker. He or she is ultimately accountable for the decision, for better or worse, and has the authority to resolve any impasse in the decision-making process and to commit the organization to action.

Perform

Once a decision is made, a person or group of people will be responsible for executing it. In some instances, the people responsible for implementing a decision are the same people who recommended it.

Writing down the roles and assigning accountability are essential steps, but good decision making also requires the right process. Too many rules can cause the process to collapse under its own weight. The most effective process is grounded in specifics but simple enough to adapt if necessary.

When the process gets slowed down, the problem can often be traced back to one of three trouble spots. First is a lack of clarity about who has the D. If more than one person think they have it for a particular decision, that decision will get caught up in a tug-of-war. The flip side can be equally damaging: No one is accountable for crucial decisions, and the business suffers. Second, a proliferation of people who have veto power can make life tough for recommenders. If a company has too many people in the "agree" role, it usually means that decisions are not pushed down far enough in the organization. Third, if there are a lot of people giving input, it's a signal that at least some of them aren't making a meaningful contribution.

Eventually, one person will *decide*. The decision maker is the single point of accountability who must bring the decision to closure and commit the organization to act on it. To be strong and effective, the person with the D needs good business judgment, a grasp of the relevant trade-offs, a bias for action, and a keen awareness of the organization that will execute the decision.

The final role in the process involves the people who will *perform* the decision. They see to it that the decision is implemented promptly and effectively. It's a crucial role. Very often, a good decision executed quickly beats a brilliant decision implemented slowly or poorly.

RAPID can be used to help redesign the way an organization works or to target a single bottleneck. Some companies use the approach for the top ten to 20 decisions, or just for the CEO and his or her direct reports. Other companies use it throughout the organization—to improve customer service by clarifying decision roles on the front line, for instance. When people see an effective process for making decisions, they spread the word. For example, after senior managers at a major U.S. retailer used RAPID to sort out a particularly thorny set of corporate decisions, they promptly built the process into their own functional organizations.

To see the process in action, let's look at the way four companies have worked through their decision-making bottlenecks.

Global Versus Local

Every major company today operates in global markets, buying raw materials in one place, shipping them somewhere else, and selling finished products all over the world. Most are trying simultaneously to build local presence and expertise, and to achieve economies of scale. Decision making in this environment is far from straightforward. Frequently, decisions cut across the boundaries between global and local managers, and sometimes across a regional layer in between: What investments will streamline our supply chain? How far should we go in standardizing products or tailoring them for local markets?

The trick in decision making is to avoid becoming either mindlessly global or hopelessly local. If decision-making authority tilts too far toward global executives, local customers' preferences can easily be overlooked, undermining the efficiency and agility of local operations. But with too much local authority, a company is likely to miss out on crucial economies of scale or opportunities with global clients.

To strike the right balance, a company must recognize its most important sources of value and make sure that decision roles line up with them. This was the challenge facing Martin Broughton, the former CEO and chairman of British American Tobacco, the second-largest tobacco company in the world. In 1993, when Broughton was appointed chief executive, BAT was losing ground to its nearest competitor. Broughton knew that the company needed to take better advantage of its global scale, but decision roles and responsibilities were at odds with this goal. Four geographic operating units ran themselves autonomously, rarely collaborating and sometimes even competing. Achieving consistency across global brands proved difficult, and cost synergies across the operating units were elusive. Industry insiders joked that "there are seven major tobacco companies in the world—and four of them are British American Tobacco." Broughton vowed to change the punch line.

The chief executive envisioned an organization that could take advantage of the opportunities a global business offers—global brands that could compete with established winners such as Altria Group's Marlboro; global purchasing of important raw materials, including tobacco; and more consistency in innovation and customer management. But Broughton didn't want the company to lose its nimbleness and competitive hunger in local markets by shifting too much decision-making power to global executives.

The first step was to clarify roles for the most important decisions. Procurement became a proving ground. Previously, each operating unit had identified its own suppliers and negotiated contracts for all materials. Under Broughton, a global procurement team was set up in headquarters and given authority to choose suppliers and negotiate pricing and quality for global materials, including bulk tobacco and certain types of packaging. Regional procurement teams were now given input into global materials strategies but ultimately had to implement the team's decision. As soon as the global team signed contracts with suppliers, responsibility shifted to the regional teams, who worked out the details of delivery and service with the suppliers in their regions. For materials that did not offer global economies of scale (mentholated filters for the North American market, for example), the regional teams retained their decision-making authority.

As the effort to revamp decision making in procurement gained momentum, the company set out to clarify roles in all its major decisions. The process wasn't easy. A company the size of British American Tobacco has a huge number of moving parts, and developing a practical system for making decisions requires sweating lots of details. What's more, decision-making authority is power, and people are often reluctant to give it up.

It's crucial for the people who will live with the new system to help design it. At BAT, Broughton created working groups led by people earmarked, implicitly or explicitly, for leadership roles in the future. For example, Paul Adams, who ultimately succeeded Broughton as chief executive, was asked to lead the group charged with redesigning decision making for brand and customer management. At the time, Adams was a regional head within one of the operating units. With other senior executives, including some of his own direct reports, Broughton specified that their role was to provide input, not to veto recommendations. Broughton didn't make the common mistake of seeking consensus, which is often an obstacle to action. Instead, he made it clear that the objective was not deciding whether to change the decision-making process but achieving buy in about how to do so as effectively as possible.

The new decision roles provided the foundation the company needed to operate successfully on a global basis while retaining flexibility at the local level. The focus and efficiency of its decision making were reflected in the company's results: After the decision-making overhaul, British American Tobacco experienced nearly ten years of growth well above the levels of its competitors in sales, profits, and market value. The company has gone on to have one of the best-performing stocks on the UK market and has reemerged as a major global player in the tobacco industry.

Center Versus Business Unit

The first rule for making good decisions is to involve the right people at the right level of the organization. For BAT, capturing economies of scale required its global team to appropriate some decision-making powers from regional divisions. For many companies, a similar balancing act takes place between executives at the center and managers in the business units. If too many decisions flow to the center, decision making can grind to a halt. The problem is different but no less critical if the decisions that are elevated to senior executives are the wrong ones.

Companies often grow into this type of problem. In small and midsize organizations, a single management team—sometimes a single leader—effectively handles every major decision. As a company grows and its operations become more complex, however, senior executives can no longer master the details required to make decisions in every business.

A change in management style, often triggered by the arrival of a new CEO, can create similar tensions. At a large British retailer, for example, the senior team was accustomed to the founder making all critical decisions. When his successor began seeking consensus on important issues, the team was suddenly unsure of its role, and many decisions stalled. It's a common scenario, yet most management teams and boards of directors don't specify how decision-making authority should change as the company does.

A growth opportunity highlighted that issue for Wyeth (then known as American Home Products) in late 2000. Through organic growth, acquisitions, and partnerships, Wyeth's pharmaceutical division had developed three sizable businesses: biotech, vaccines, and traditional pharmaceutical products. Even though each business had its own market dynamics, operating requirements, and research focus, most important decisions were pushed up to one group of senior executives. "We were using generalists across all issues," said Joseph M. Mahady, president of North American and global businesses for Wyeth Pharmaceuticals. "It was a signal that we weren't getting our best decision making."

The problem crystallized for Wyeth when managers in the biotech business saw a vital—but perishable—opportunity to establish a leading position with Enbrel, a promising rheumatoid arthritis drug. Competitors were working on the same class of drug, so Wyeth needed to move quickly. This meant expanding production capacity by building a new plant, which would be located at the Grange Castle Business Park in Dublin, Ireland.

The decision, by any standard, was a complex one. Once approved by regulators, the facility would be the biggest biotech plant in the world—and the largest capital investment Wyeth had ever undertaken. Yet peak demand for the drug was not easy to determine. What's more, Wyeth planned to market Enbrel in partnership with Immunex (now a part of Amgen). In its deliberations about the plant, therefore, Wyeth needed to factor in the requirements of building up its technical expertise, technology transfer issues, and an uncertain competitive environment.

Input on the decision filtered up slowly through a gauze of overlapping committees, leaving senior executives hungry for a more detailed grasp of the issues. Given the narrow window of opportunity, Wyeth acted quickly, moving from a first look at the Grange Castle project to implementation in six months. But in the midst of this process, Wyeth Pharmaceuticals' executives saw the larger issue: The company needed a system that would push more decisions down to the business units, where operational knowledge was greatest, and elevate the decisions that required the senior team's input, such as marketing strategy and manufacturing capacity.

In short order, Wyeth gave authority for many decisions to business unit managers, leaving senior executives with veto power over some of the more sensitive issues related to Grange Castle. But after that investment decision was made, the D for many subsequent decisions about the Enbrel business lay with Cavan Redmond, the executive vice president and general manager of Wyeth's biotech division, and his new management team. Redmond gathered input from managers in biotech manufacturing, marketing, forecasting, finance, and R&D, and quickly set up the complex schedules needed to collaborate with Immunex. Responsibility for execution rested firmly with the business unit, as always. But now Redmond, supported by his team, also had authority to make important decisions.

Grange Castle is paying off so far. Enbrel is among the leading brands for rheumatoid arthritis, with sales of $1.7 billion through the first half of 2005. And Wyeth's metabolism for making decisions has increased. Recently, when the U.S. Food and Drug Administration granted priority review status to another new drug, Tygacil, because of the antibiotic's efficacy against drug-resistant infections, Wyeth displayed its new reflexes. To keep Tygacil on a fast track, the company had to orchestrate a host of critical steps—refining the process technology, lining up supplies, ensuring quality control, allocating manufacturing capacity. The vital decisions were made one or two levels down in the biotech organization, where the expertise resided. "Instead of debating whether you can move your product into my shop, we had the decision systems in place to run it up and down the business units and move ahead rapidly with Tygacil," said Mahady. The drug was approved by the FDA in June 2005 and moved into volume production a mere three days later.

Function Versus Function

Decisions that cut across functions are some of the most important a company faces. Indeed, cross-functional collaboration has become an axiom of business, essential for arriving at the best answers for the company and its customers. But fluid decision making across functional teams remains a constant challenge, even for companies known for doing it well, like Toyota and Dell. For instance, a team that thinks it's more efficient to make a decision without consulting other functions may wind up missing out on relevant input or being overruled by another team that believes—rightly or wrongly—it should have been included in the process. Many of the most important cross-functional decisions are, by their very nature, the most difficult to orchestrate, and that can string out the process and lead to sparring between fiefdoms and costly indecision.

The theme here is a lack of clarity about who has the D. For example, at a global auto manufacturer that was missing its milestones for rolling out new models—and was paying the price in falling sales—it turned out that marketers and product developers were confused about which function was responsible for making decisions about standard features and color ranges for new models. When we asked the marketing team who had the D about which features should be standard, 83% said the marketers did. When we

---

A recipe for a decision-making bottleneck

At one automaker we studied, marketers and product developers were confused about who was responsible for making decisions about new models.

When we asked, "Who has the right to decide which features will be standard?"

- 64% of product developers said, "We do."
- 83% of marketers said, "We do."

Not surprisingly, the new models were delayed.

When we asked, "Who has the right to decide which colors will be offered?"

- 77% of product developers said, "We do."
- 61% of marketers said, "We do."

---

posed the same question to product developers, 64% said the responsibility rested with them. (See the exhibit "A recipe for a decision-making bottleneck.")

The practical difficulty of connecting functions through smooth decision making crops up frequently at retailers. John Lewis, the leading department store chain in the United Kingdom, might reasonably expect to overcome this sort of challenge more readily than other retailers. Spedan Lewis, who built the business in the early twentieth century, was a pioneer in employee ownership. A strong connection between managers and employees permeated every aspect of the store's operations and remained vital to the company as it grew into the largest employee-owned business in the United Kingdom, with 59,600 employees and more than £5 billion in revenues in 2004.

Even at John Lewis, however, with its heritage of cooperation and teamwork, cross-functional decision making can be hard to sustain. Take salt and pepper mills, for instance. John Lewis, which prides itself on having great selection, stocked nearly 50 SKUs of salt and pepper mills, while most competitors stocked around 20. The company's buyers saw an opportunity to increase sales and reduce complexity by offering a smaller number of popular and well-chosen products in each price point and style.

When John Lewis launched the new range, sales fell. This made no sense to the buyers until they visited the stores and saw how the merchandise was displayed. The buyers had made their decision without fully involving the sales staff, who therefore did not understand the strategy behind the new selection. As a result, the sellers had cut shelf space in half to match the reduction in range, rather than devoting the same amount of shelf space to stocking more of each product.

To fix the communication problem, John Lewis needed to clarify decision roles. The buyers were given the D on how much space to allocate to each product category. If the space allocation didn't make sense to the sales staff, however, they had the authority to raise their concerns and force a new round of negotiations. They also had responsibility for implementing product layouts in the stores. When the communication was sorted out and shelf space was restored, sales of the salt and pepper mills climbed well above original levels.

Crafting a decision-making process that connected the buying and selling functions for salt and pepper mills was relatively easy; rolling it out across the entire business was more challenging. Salt and pepper mills are just one of several hundred product categories for John Lewis. This element of scale is one reason why cross-functional bottlenecks are not easy to unclog. Different functions have different incentives and goals, which are often in conflict. When it comes down to a struggle between two functions, there may be good reasons to locate the D in either place—buying or selling, marketing or product development.

Here, as elsewhere, someone needs to think objectively about where value is created and assign decision roles accordingly. Eliminating cross-functional bottlenecks actually has less to do with shifting decision-making responsibilities between departments and more to do with ensuring that the people with relevant information are allowed to share it. The decision maker is important, of course, but more important is designing a system that aligns decision making and makes it routine.

Inside Versus Outside Partners

Decision making within an organization is hard enough. Trying to make decisions between separate organizations on different continents adds

The Decision-Driven Organization

THE DEFINING CHARACTERISTIC OF HIGH-PERFORMING organizations is their ability to make good decisions and to make them happen quickly. The companies that succeed tend to follow a few clear principles.

Some Decisions Matter More Than Others
The decisions that are crucial to building value in the business are the ones that matter most. Some of them will be the big strategic decisions, but just as important are the critical operating decisions that drive the business day to day and are vital to effective execution.

Action Is the Goal
Good decision making doesn't end with a decision; it ends with implementation. The objective shouldn't be consensus, which often becomes an obstacle to action, but buy in.

Ambiguity Is the Enemy
Clear accountability is essential: Who contributes input, who makes the decision, and who carries it out? Without clarity, gridlock and delay are the most likely outcomes. Clarity doesn't necessarily mean concentrating authority in a few people; it means defining who has responsibility to make decisions, who has input, and who is charged with putting them into action.

---

layers of complexity that can scuttle the best strategy. Companies that outsource capabilities in pursuit of cost and quality advantages face this very challenge. Which decisions should be made internally? Which can be delegated to outsourcing partners?

These questions are also relevant for strategic partners—a global bank working with an IT contractor on a systems development project, for example, or a media company that acquires content from a studio—and for companies conducting part of their business through franchisees. There is no right answer to who should have the power to decide what. But the wrong approach is to assume that contractual arrangements can provide the answer.

An outdoor-equipment company based in the United States discovered this recently when it decided to scale up production of gas patio heaters for the lower end of the market. The company had some success manufacturing high-end products in China. But with

Speed and Adaptability Are Crucial

A company that makes good decisions quickly has a higher metabolism, which allows it to act on opportunities and overcome obstacles. The best decision makers create an environment where people can come together quickly and efficiently to make the most important decisions.

Decision Roles Trump the Organizational Chart

No decision-making structure will be perfect for every decision. The key is to involve the right people at the right level in the right part of the organization at the right time.

A Well-Aligned Organization Reinforces Roles

Clear decision roles are critical, but they are not enough. If an organization does not reinforce the right approach to decision making through its measures and incentives, information flows, and culture, the behavior won't become routine.

Practicing Beats Preaching

Involve the people who will live with the new decision roles in designing them. The very process of thinking about new decision behaviors motivates people to adopt them.

---

the advent of superdiscounters like Wal-Mart, Target, and Home Depot, the company realized it needed to move more of its production overseas to feed these retailers with lower-cost offerings. The timetable left little margin for error: The company started tooling up factories in April and June of 2004, hoping to be ready for the Christmas season.

Right away, there were problems. Although the Chinese manufacturing partners understood costs, they had little idea what American consumers wanted. When expensive designs arrived from the head office in the United States, Chinese plant managers made compromises to meet contracted cost targets. They used a lower grade material, which discolored. They placed the power switch in a spot that was inconvenient for the user but easier to build. Instead of making certain parts from a single casting, they welded materials together, which looked terrible.

A Decision Diagnostic

CONSIDER THE LAST THREE MEANINGFUL decisions you've been involved in and ask yourself the following questions.

1. Were the decisions right?

2. Were they made with appropriate speed?

3. Were they executed well?

4. Were the right people involved, in the right way?

5. Was it clear for each decision

   • who would recommend a solution?

   • who would provide input?

   • who had the final say?

   • who would be responsible for following through?

6. Were the decision roles, process, and time frame respected?

7. Were the decisions based on appropriate facts?

8. To the extent that there were divergent facts or opinions, was it clear who had the D?

9. Were the decision makers at the appropriate level in the company?

10. Did the organization's measures and incentives encourage the people involved to make the right decisions?

To fix these problems, the U.S. executives had to draw clear lines around which decisions should be made on which side of the ocean. The company broke down the design and manufacturing process into five steps and analyzed how decisions were made at each step. The company was also much more explicit about what the manufacturing specs would include and what the manufacturer was expected to do with them. The objective was not simply to clarify decision roles but to make sure those roles corresponded directly to the sources of value in the business. If a decision would affect the look and feel of the finished product, headquarters would have to sign off on it. But if a decision would not affect the customer's experience, it could be made in China. If, for example, Chinese engineers found a less expensive material that didn't compromise the product's look, feel, and functionality, they could make that change on their own.

To help with the transition to this system, the company put a team of engineers on-site in China to ensure a smooth handoff of the specs and to make decisions on issues that would become complex and time-consuming if elevated to the home office. Marketing executives in the home office insisted that it should take a customer ten minutes and no more than six steps to assemble the product at home. The company's engineers in China, along with the Chinese manufacturing team, had input into this assembly requirement and were responsible for execution. But the D resided with headquarters, and the requirement became a major design factor. Decisions about logistics, however, became the province of the engineering team in China: It would figure out how to package the heaters so that one-third more boxes would fit into a container, which reduced shipping costs substantially.

If managers suddenly realize that they're spending less time sitting through meetings wondering why they are there, that's an early signal that companies have become better at making decisions. When meetings start with a common understanding about who is responsible for providing valuable input and who has the D, an organization's decision-making metabolism will get a boost.

No single lever turns a decision-challenged organization into a decision-driven one, of course, and no blueprint can provide for all the contingencies and business shifts a company is bound to encounter. The most successful companies use simple tools that help them recognize potential bottlenecks and think through decision roles and responsibilities with each change in the business environment. That's difficult to do—and even more difficult for competitors to copy. But by taking some very practical steps, any company can become more effective, beginning with its next decision.

Originally published in January 2006. Reprint R0601D

How (Un)ethical Are You?

by Mahzarin R. Banaji, Max H. Bazerman, and Dolly Chugh

ANSWER TRUE OR FALSE: "I am an ethical manager."

If you answered "true," here's an uncomfortable fact: You're probably not. Most of us believe that we are ethical and unbiased. We imagine we're good decision makers, able to objectively size up a job candidate or a venture deal and reach a fair and rational conclusion that's in our, and our organization's, best interests. But more than two decades of research confirms that, in reality, most of us fall woefully short of our inflated self-perception. We're deluded by what Yale psychologist David Armor calls the illusion of objectivity, the notion that we're free of the very biases we're so quick to recognize in others. What's more, these unconscious, or implicit, biases can be contrary to our consciously held, explicit beliefs. We may believe with confidence and conviction that a job candidate's race has no bearing on our hiring decisions or that we're immune to conflicts of interest. But psychological research routinely exposes counterintentional, unconscious biases. The prevalence of these biases suggests that even the most well-meaning person unwittingly allows unconscious thoughts and feelings to influence seemingly objective decisions. These flawed judgments are ethically problematic and undermine managers' fundamental work—to recruit and retain superior talent, boost the performance of individuals and teams, and collaborate effectively with partners.

This article explores four related sources of unintentional unethical decision making: implicit forms of prejudice, bias that favors one's own group, conflict of interest, and a tendency to overclaim credit. Because we are not consciously aware of these sources of bias, they often cannot be addressed by penalizing people for their bad decisions. Nor are they likely to be corrected through conventional ethics training. Rather, managers must bring a new type of vigilance to bear. To begin, this requires letting go of the notion that our conscious attitudes always represent what we think they do. It also demands that we abandon our faith in our own objectivity and our ability to be fair. In the following pages, we will offer strategies that can help managers recognize these pervasive, corrosive, unconscious biases and reduce their impact.

Implicit Prejudice: Bias That Emerges from Unconscious Beliefs

Most fair-minded people strive to judge others according to their merits, but our research shows how often people instead judge according to unconscious stereotypes and attitudes, or "implicit prejudice." What makes implicit prejudice so common and persistent is that it is rooted in the fundamental mechanics of thought. Early on, we learn to associate things that commonly go together and expect them to inevitably coexist: thunder and rain, for instance, or gray hair and old age. This skill—to perceive and learn from associations—often serves us well.

But, of course, our associations only reflect approximations of the truth; they are rarely applicable to every encounter. Rain doesn't always accompany thunder, and the young can also go gray. Nonetheless, because we automatically make such associations to help us organize our world, we grow to trust them, and they can blind us to those instances in which the associations are not accurate—when they don't align with our expectations.

Because implicit prejudice arises from the ordinary and unconscious tendency to make associations, it is distinct from conscious forms of prejudice, such as overt racism or sexism. This distinction

Idea in Brief

Are you an ethical manager? Most would probably say, "Of course!" The truth is, most of us are not.

Most of us believe that we're ethical and unbiased. We assume that we objectively size up job candidates or venture deals and reach fair and rational conclusions that are in our organization's best interests.

But the truth is, we harbor many unconscious—and unethical— biases that derail our decisions and undermine our work as managers. Hidden biases prevent us from recognizing high-potential workers and retaining talented managers. They stop us from collaborating effectively with partners. They erode our teams' performance. They can also lead to costly lawsuits.

But how can we root out these biases if they're unconscious? Fortunately, as a manager, you can take deliberate actions to counteract their pull. **Regularly audit your decisions.** Have you, for example, hired a disproportionate number of people of your own race? **Expose yourself to non-stereotypical environments** that challenge your biases. If your department is led by men, spend time in one with women in leadership positions. And **consider counterintuitive options** when making decisions. Don't rely on a mental short-list of candidates for a new assignment; consider every employee with relevant qualifications.

explains why people who are free from conscious prejudice may still harbor biases and act accordingly. Exposed to images that juxtapose black men and violence, portray women as sex objects, imply that the physically disabled are mentally weak and the poor are lazy, even the most consciously unbiased person is bound to make biased associations. These associations play out in the workplace just as they do anywhere else.

In the mid-1990s, Tony Greenwald, a professor of psychology at the University of Washington, developed an experimental tool called the Implicit Association Test (IAT) to study unconscious bias. A computerized version of the test requires subjects to rapidly classify words and images as "good" or "bad." Using a keyboard, test takers must make split-second "good/bad" distinctions between words like "love," "joy," "pain," and "sorrow" and at the same time sort images of faces that are (depending on the bias in question)

Idea in Practice

Unconscious Biases

Are the following unconscious biases levying what amounts to a "stereotype tax" on your company?

Implicit prejudice. Judging according to unconscious stereotypes rather than merit exacts a high business cost. Exposed to images that juxtapose physical disabilities with mental weakness or portray poor people as lazy, even the most consciously unbiased person is bound to make biased associations. As a result, we routinely overlook highly qualified candidates for assignments.

In-group favoritism. Granting favors to people with your same background—your nationality or alma mater—effectively discriminates against those who are different from you. Consider the potential cost of offering bonuses to employees who refer their friends for job openings: hires who may not have made the grade *without* in-group favoritism.

Overclaiming credit. Most of us consider ourselves above average. But when every member of a team thinks he's making the biggest contribution, each starts to think the others aren't pulling their weight. That jeopardizes future collaborations. It also frustrates talented workers who may resign because they feel underappreciated.

Counteract Biases

To keep yourself from making similarly skewed calls, consider these guidelines:

---

black or white, young or old, fat or thin, and so on. The test exposes implicit biases by detecting subtle shifts in reaction time that can occur when test takers are required to pair different sets of words and faces. Subjects who consciously believe that they have no negative feelings toward, say, black Americans or the elderly are nevertheless likely to be slower to associate elderly or black faces with the "good" words than they are to associate youthful or white faces with "good" words.

Since 1998, when Greenwald, Brian Nosek, and Mahzarin Banaji put the IAT online, people from around the world have taken over 2.5 million tests, confirming and extending the findings of more traditional laboratory experiments. Both show implicit biases to

Gather better data. Expose your own implicit biases. Take the Implicit Association Test (at http://implicit.harvard. edu). If you discover gender or racial biases, examine your hiring and promotion decisions in that new light. When working with others, have team members estimate their colleagues' contributions *before* they claim their own credit.

Rid your workplace of stereotypical cues. Think about the biased associations your workplace may foster. Do your company's advertising and marketing materials frequently include sports metaphors or high-tech jargon? Make a conscious effort to curb such "insider" language—making your products more appealing to a diverse customer base. And if your department invariably promotes the same type of manager—highly analytic, for instance—shadow a department that values a different—perhaps more conceptual—skill-set.

Broaden your mind-set when making decisions. Apply the "veil of ignorance" to your next managerial decision. Suppose you're considering a new policy that would give more vacation time to all employees but eliminate the flextime that has allowed new parents to keep working. How would your opinion differ if you were a parent or childless? Male or female? Healthy or unhealthy? You'll learn how strongly implicit biases influence you.

be strong and pervasive. (For more information on the IAT, see the sidebar "Are You Biased?").

Biases are also likely to be costly. In controlled experiments, psychologists Laurie Rudman at Rutgers and Peter Glick at Lawrence University have studied how implicit biases may work to exclude qualified people from certain roles. One set of experiments examined the relationship between participants' implicit gender stereotypes and their hiring decisions. Those holding stronger implicit biases were less likely to select a qualified woman who exhibited stereotypically "masculine" personality qualities, such as ambition or independence, for a job requiring stereotypically "feminine" qualities, such as interpersonal skills. Yet they would select a qualified man

Are You Biased?

ARE YOU WILLING TO BET that you feel the same way toward European-Americans as you do toward African-Americans? How about women versus men? Or older people versus younger ones? Think twice before you take that bet. Visit implicit.harvard.edu or www.tolerance.org/hidden_bias to examine your unconscious attitudes.

The Implicit Association Tests available on these sites reveal unconscious beliefs by asking takers to make split-second associations between words with positive or negative connotations and images representing different types of people. The various tests on these sites expose the differences—or the alignment—between test takers' conscious and unconscious attitudes toward people of different races, sexual orientation, or physical characteristics. Data gathered from over 2.5 million online tests and further research tells us that unconscious biases are:

- **widely prevalent.** At least 75% of test takers show an implicit bias favoring the young, the rich, and whites.

- **robust.** The mere conscious desire not to be biased does not eliminate implicit bias.

- **contrary to conscious intention.** Although people tend to report little or no *conscious* bias against African-Americans, Arabs, Arab-Americans, Jews, gay men, lesbians, or the poor, they show substantial biases on implicit measures.

- **different in degree depending on group status.** Minority group members tend to show less implicit preference for their own group than majority group members show for theirs. For example, African-Americans report strong preference for their group on explicit measures but show relatively less implicit preference in the tests. Conversely, white Americans report a low explicit bias for their group but a higher implicit bias.

- **consequential.** Those who show higher levels of bias on the IAT are also likely to behave in ways that are more biased in face-to-face interactions with members of the group they are biased against and in the choices they make, such as hiring decisions.

- **costly.** Research currently under way in our lab suggests that implicit bias generates a "stereotype tax"—negotiators leave money on the table because biases cause them to miss opportunities to learn about their opponent and thus create additional value through mutually beneficial trade-offs.

exhibiting these same qualities. The hirers' biased perception was that the woman was less likely to be socially skilled than the man, though their qualifications were in fact the same. These results suggest that implicit biases may exact costs by subtly excluding qualified people from the very organizations that seek their talents.

Legal cases also reveal the real costs of implicit biases, both economic and social. Consider *Price Waterhouse v. Hopkins*. Despite logging more billable hours than her peers, bringing in $25 million to the company, and earning the praise of her clients, Ann Hopkins was turned down for partner, and she sued. The details of the case reveal that her evaluators were explicitly prejudiced in their attitudes. For example, they had commented that Ann "overcompensated for being a woman" and needed a "course at charm school." But perhaps more damning from a legal standpoint was blunt testimony from experimental research. Testifying as an expert witness for the defense, psychology professor Susan Fiske, now at Princeton University, argued that the potential for biased decision making is *inherent* in a system in which a person has "solo" status—that is, a system in which the person is the only one of a kind (the only woman, the only African-American, the only person with a disability, and the like). Judge Gerhard Gesell concluded that "a far more subtle process [than the usual discriminatory intent] is involved" in the assessments made of Ann Hopkins, and she won both in a lower court and in the Supreme Court in what is now a landmark case in discrimination law.

Likewise, the 1999 case of *Thomas v. Kodak* demonstrates that implicit biases can be the basis for rulings. Here, the court posed the question of "whether the employer consciously intended to base the evaluations on race or simply did so because of unthinking stereotypes or bias." The court concluded that plaintiffs can indeed challenge "subjective evaluations which could easily mask covert or unconscious race discrimination." Although courts are careful not to assign responsibility easily for unintentional biases, these cases demonstrate the potential for corporate liability that such patterns of behavior could unwittingly create.

In-Group Favoritism: Bias That Favors Your Group

Think about some of the favors you have done in recent years, whether for a friend, a relative, or a colleague. Have you helped someone get a useful introduction, admission to a school, or a job? Most of us are glad to help out with such favors. Not surprisingly, we tend to do more favors for those we know, and those we know tend to be like ourselves: people who share our nationality, social class, and perhaps religion, race, employer, or alma mater. This all sounds rather innocent. What's wrong with asking your neighbor, the university dean, to meet with a coworker's son? Isn't it just being helpful to recommend a former sorority sister for a job or to talk to your banker cousin when a friend from church gets turned down for a home loan?

Few people set out to exclude anyone through such acts of kindness. But when those in the majority or those in power allocate scarce resources (such as jobs, promotions, and mortgages) to people just like them, they effectively discriminate against those who are different from them. Such "in-group favoritism" amounts to giving extra credit for group membership. Yet while discriminating against those who are different is considered unethical, helping people close to us is often viewed favorably. Think about the number of companies that explicitly encourage this by offering hiring bonuses to employees who refer their friends for job opportunities.

But consider the finding that banks in the United States are more likely to deny a mortgage application from a black person than from a white person, even when the applicants are equally qualified. The common view has been that banks are hostile to African-Americans. While this may be true of some banks and some loan officers, social psychologist David Messick has argued that in-group favoritism is more likely to be at the root of such discriminatory lending. A white loan officer may feel hopeful or lenient toward an unqualified white applicant while following the bank's lending standards strictly with an unqualified black applicant. In denying the black applicant's mortgage, the loan officer may not be expressing hostility toward blacks so much as favoritism toward whites. It's a subtle but crucial distinction.

The ethical cost is clear and should be reason enough to address the problem. But such inadvertent bias produces an additional effect: It erodes the bottom line. Lenders who discriminate in this way, for example, incur bad-debt costs they could have avoided if their lending decisions were more objective. They also may find themselves exposed to damaging publicity or discrimination lawsuits if the skewed lending pattern is publicly revealed. In a different context, companies may pay a real cost for marginal hires who wouldn't have made the grade but for the sympathetic hiring manager swayed by in-group favoritism.

In-group favoritism is tenacious when membership confers clear advantages, as it does, for instance, among whites and other dominant social groups. (It may be weaker or absent among people whose group membership offers little societal advantage.) Thus for a wide array of managerial tasks—from hiring, firing, and promoting to contracting services and forming partnerships—qualified minority candidates are subtly and unconsciously discriminated against, sometimes simply because they are in the minority: There are not enough of them to counter the propensity for in-group favoritism in the majority.

Overclaiming Credit: Bias That Favors You

It's only natural for successful people to hold positive views about themselves. But many studies show that the majority of people consider themselves above average on a host of measures, from intelligence to driving ability. Business executives are no exception. We tend to overrate our individual contribution to groups, which, bluntly put, tends to lead to an overblown sense of entitlement. We become the unabashed, repeated beneficiaries of this unconscious bias, and the more we think only of our own contributions, the less fairly we judge others with whom we work.

Lab research demonstrates this most personal of biases. At Harvard, Eugene Caruso, Nick Epley, and Max Bazerman recently asked MBA students in study groups to estimate what portion of their group's work each had done. The sum of the contribution by all members, of course, must add up to 100%. But the researchers found that the totals for each study group averaged 139%. In a related study, Caruso and his colleagues uncovered rampant overestimates by academic authors of their contribution to shared research projects. Sadly, but not surprisingly, the more the sum of the total estimated group effort exceeded 100% (in other words, the more credit each person claimed), the less the parties wanted to collaborate in the future.

Likewise in business, claiming too much credit can destabilize alliances. When each party in a strategic partnership claims too much credit for its own contribution and becomes skeptical about whether the other is doing its fair share, they both tend to reduce their contributions to compensate. This has obvious repercussions for the joint venture's performance.

Unconscious overclaiming can be expected to reduce the performance and longevity of groups within organizations, just as it diminished the academic authors' willingness to collaborate. It can also take a toll on employee commitment. Think about how employees perceive raises. Most are not so different from the children at Lake Wobegon, believing that they, too, rank in the upper half of their peer group. But many necessarily get pay increases that are below the average. If an employee learns of a colleague's greater compensation—while honestly believing that he himself is more deserving—resentment may be natural. At best, his resentment might translate into reduced commitment and performance. At worst, he may leave the organization that, it seems, doesn't appreciate his contribution.

Conflict of Interest: Bias That Favors Those Who Can Benefit You

Everyone knows that conflict of interest can lead to intentionally corrupt behavior. But numerous psychological experiments show how powerfully such conflicts can unintentionally skew decision making. (For an examination of the evidence in one business arena, see Max Bazerman, George Loewenstein, and Don Moore's November 2002

HBR article, "Why Good Accountants Do Bad Audits.") These experiments suggest that the work world is rife with situations in which such conflicts lead honest, ethical professionals to unconsciously make unsound and unethical recommendations.

Physicians, for instance, face conflicts of interest when they accept payment for referring patients into clinical trials. While, surely, most physicians consciously believe that their referrals are the patient's best clinical option, how do they know that the promise of payment did not skew their decisions? Similarly, many lawyers earn fees based on their clients' awards or settlements. Since going to trial is expensive and uncertain, settling out of court is often an attractive option for the lawyer. Attorneys may consciously believe that settling is in their clients' best interests. But how can they be objective, unbiased judges under these circumstances?

Research done with brokerage house analysts demonstrates how conflict of interest can unconsciously distort decision making. A survey of analysts conducted by the financial research service First Call showed that during a period in 2000 when the Nasdaq dropped 60%, fully 99% of brokerage analysts' client recommendations remained "strong buy," "buy," or "hold." What accounts for this discrepancy between what was happening and what was recommended? The answer may lie in a system that fosters conflicts of interest. A portion of analysts' pay is based on brokerage firm revenues. Some firms even tie analysts' compensation to the amount of business the analysts bring in from clients, giving analysts an obvious incentive to prolong and extend their relationships with clients. But to assume that during this Nasdaq free fall all brokerage house analysts were consciously corrupt, milking their clients to exploit this incentive system, defies common sense. Surely there were some bad apples. But how much more likely it is that most of these analysts believed their recommendations were sound and in their clients' best interests. What many didn't appreciate was that the built-in conflict of interest in their compensation incentives made it impossible for them to see the implicit bias in their own flawed recommendations.

Trying Harder Isn't Enough

As companies keep collapsing into financial scandal and ruin, corporations are responding with ethics-training programs for managers, and many of the world's leading business schools have created new courses and chaired professorships in ethics. Many of these efforts focus on teaching broad principles of moral philosophy to help managers understand the ethical challenges they face.

We applaud these efforts, but we doubt that a well-intentioned, just-try-harder approach will fundamentally improve the quality of executives' decision making. To do that, ethics training must be broadened to include what is now known about how our minds work and must expose managers directly to the unconscious mechanisms that underlie biased decision making. And it must provide managers with exercises and interventions that can root out the biases that lead to bad decisions.

Managers can make wiser, more ethical decisions if they become mindful of their unconscious biases. But how can we get at something outside our conscious awareness? By bringing the conscious mind to bear. Just as the driver of a misaligned car deliberately counteracts its pull, so can managers develop conscious strategies to counteract the pull of their unconscious biases. What's required is vigilance—continual awareness of the forces that can cause decision making to veer from its intended course and continual adjustments to counteract them. Those adjustments fall into three general categories: collecting data, shaping the environment, and broadening the decision-making process.

Collect data

The first step to reducing unconscious bias is to collect data to reveal its presence. Often, the data will be counterintuitive. Consider many people's surprise to learn of their own gender and racial biases on the IAT. Why the surprise? Because most of us trust the "statistics" our intuition provides. Better data are easily, but rarely, collected. One way to get those data is to examine our decisions in a systematic way.

Remember the MBA study groups whose participants overestimated their individual contributions to the group effort so that the totals averaged 139%? When the researchers asked group members to estimate what each of the other members' contributions were *before* claiming their own, the total fell to 121%. The tendency to claim too much credit still persisted, but this strategy of "unpacking" the work reduced the magnitude of the bias. In environments characterized by "I deserve more than you're giving me" claims, merely asking team members to unpack the contributions of others before claiming their own share of the pot usually aligns claims more closely with what's actually deserved. As this example demonstrates, such systematic audits of both individual and group decision-making processes can occur even as the decisions are being made.

Unpacking is a simple strategy that managers should routinely use to evaluate the fairness of their own claims within the organization. But they can also apply it in any situation where team members or subordinates may be overclaiming. For example, in explaining a raise that an employee feels is inadequate, a manager should ask the subordinate not what he thinks he alone deserves but what he considers an appropriate raise after taking into account each coworker's contribution and the pool available for pay increases. Similarly, when an individual feels she's doing more than her fair share of a team's work, asking her to consider other people's efforts before estimating her own can help align her perception with reality, restore her commitment, and reduce a skewed sense of entitlement.

Taking the IAT is another valuable strategy for collecting data. We recommend that you and others in your organization use the test to expose your own implicit biases. But one word of warning: Because the test is an educational and research tool, not a selection or evaluation tool, it is critical that you consider your results and others' to be private information. Simply knowing the magnitude and pervasiveness of your own biases can help direct your attention to areas of decision making that are in need of careful examination and reconsideration. For example, a manager whose testing reveals a bias toward certain groups ought to examine her hiring practices to see if she has indeed been disproportionately favoring those groups. But because so many people harbor such biases, they can also be generally acknowledged, and that knowledge can be used as the basis for changing the way decisions are made. It is important to guard against using pervasiveness to justify complacency and inaction: Pervasiveness of bias is not a mark of its appropriateness any more than poor eyesight is considered so ordinary a condition that it does not require corrective lenses.

Shape your environment

Research shows that implicit attitudes can be shaped by external cues in the environment. For example, Curtis Hardin and colleagues at UCLA used the IAT to study whether subjects' implicit race bias would be affected if the test was administered by a black investigator. One group of students took the test under the guidance of a white experimenter; another group took the test with a black experimenter. The mere presence of a black experimenter, Hardin found, reduced the level of subjects' implicit antiblack bias on the IAT. Numerous similar studies have shown similar effects with other social groups. What accounts for such shifts? We can speculate that experimenters in classrooms are assumed to be competent, in charge, and authoritative. Subjects guided by a black experimenter attribute these positive characteristics to that person, and then perhaps to the group as a whole. These findings suggest that one remedy for implicit bias is to expose oneself to images and social environments that challenge stereotypes.

We know of a judge whose court is located in a predominantly African-American neighborhood. Because of the crime and arrest patterns in the community, most people the judge sentences are black. The judge confronted a paradox. On the one hand, she took a judicial oath to be objective and egalitarian, and indeed she consciously believed that her decisions were unbiased. On the other hand, every day she was exposed to an environment that reinforced the association between black men and crime. Although she consciously rejected racial stereotypes, she suspected that she harbored unconscious prejudices merely from working in a segregated world.

Immersed in this environment each day, she wondered if it was possible to give the defendants a fair hearing.

Rather than allow her environment to reinforce a bias, the judge created an alternative environment. She spent a vacation week sitting in a fellow judge's court in a neighborhood where the criminals being tried were predominantly white. Case after case challenged the stereotype of blacks as criminal and whites as law abiding and so challenged any bias against blacks that she might have harbored.

Think about the possibly biased associations your workplace fosters. Is there, perhaps, a "wall of fame" with pictures of high achievers all cast from the same mold? Are certain types of managers invariably promoted? Do people overuse certain analogies drawn from stereotypical or narrow domains of knowledge (sports metaphors, for instance, or cooking terms)? Managers can audit their organization to uncover such patterns or cues that unwittingly lead to stereotypical associations.

If an audit reveals that the environment may be promoting unconscious biased or unethical behavior, consider creating countervailing experiences, as the judge did. For example, if your department reinforces the stereotype of men as naturally dominant in a hierarchy (most managers are male, and most assistants are female), find a department with women in leadership positions and set up a shadow program. Both groups will benefit from the exchange of best practices, and your group will be quietly exposed to counterstereotypical cues. Managers sending people out to spend time in clients' organizations as a way to improve service should take care to select organizations likely to counter stereotypes reinforced in your own company.

Broaden your decision making

Imagine that you are making a decision in a meeting about an important company policy that will benefit some groups of employees more than others. A policy might, for example, provide extra vacation time for all employees but eliminate the flex time that has allowed many new parents to balance work with their family responsibilities. Another policy might lower the mandatory retirement age, eliminating some older workers but creating advancement opportunities for younger ones. Now pretend that, as you make your decisions, you don't know which group you belong to. That is, you don't know whether you are senior or junior, married or single, gay or straight, a parent or childless, male or female, healthy or unhealthy. You will eventually find out, but not until after the decision has been made. In this hypothetical scenario, what decision would you make? Would you be willing to risk being in the group disadvantaged by your own decision? How would your decisions differ if you could make them wearing various identities not your own?

This thought experiment is a version of philosopher John Rawls's concept of the "veil of ignorance," which posits that only a person ignorant of his own identity is capable of a truly ethical decision. Few of us can assume the veil completely, which is precisely why hidden biases, even when identified, are so difficult to correct. Still, applying the veil of ignorance to your next important managerial decision may offer some insight into how strongly implicit biases influence you.

Just as managers can expose bias by collecting data before acting on intuition, they can take other preemptive steps. What list of names do you start with when considering whom to send to a training program, recommend for a new assignment, or nominate for a fast-track position? Most of us can quickly and with little concentration come up with such a list. But keep in mind that your intuition is prone to implicit prejudice (which will strongly favor dominant and well-liked groups), in-group favoritism (which will favor people in your own group), overclaiming (which will favor you), and conflict of interest (which will favor people whose interests affect your own). Instead of relying on a mental short list when making personnel decisions, start with a full list of names of employees who have relevant qualifications.

Using a broad list of names has several advantages. The most obvious is that talent may surface that might otherwise be overlooked. Less obvious but equally important, the very act of considering a counterstereotypical choice at the conscious level can reduce implicit bias. In fact, merely thinking about hypothetical, counterstereotypical scenarios—such as what it would be like to trust a complex presentation to a female colleague or to receive a promotion from an African-American boss—can prompt less-biased and more ethical decision making. Similarly, consciously considering counterintuitive options in the face of conflicts of interest, or when there's an opportunity to over-claim, can promote more objective and ethical decisions.

The Vigilant Manager

If you answered "true" to the question at the start of this article, you felt with some confidence that you are an ethical decision maker. How would you answer it now? It's clear that neither simple conviction nor sincere intention is enough to ensure that you are the ethical practitioner you imagine yourself to be. Managers who aspire to be ethical must challenge the assumption that they're always unbiased and acknowledge that vigilance, even more than good intention, is a defining characteristic of an ethical manager. They must actively collect data, shape their environments, and broaden their decision making. What's more, an obvious redress is available. Managers should seek every opportunity to implement affirmative action policies—not because of past wrongs done to one group or another but because of the everyday wrongs that we can now document are inherent in the ordinary, everyday behavior of good, well-intentioned people. Ironically, only those who understand their own potential for unethical behavior can become the ethical decision makers that they aspire to be.

Originally published in December 2003. Reprint R0312D

Make Better Decisions

by Thomas H. Davenport

IN RECENT YEARS DECISION MAKERS in both the public and private sectors have made an astounding number of poor calls. For example, the decisions to invade Iraq, not to comply with global warming treaties, to ignore Darfur, are all likely to be recorded as injudicious in history books. And how about the decisions to invest in and securitize subprime mortgage loans, or to hedge risk with credit default swaps? Those were spread across a number of companies, but single organizations, too, made bad decisions. Tenneco, once a large conglomerate, chose poorly when buying businesses and now consists of only one auto parts business. General Motors made terrible decisions about which cars to bring to market. Time Warner erred in buying AOL, and Yahoo in deciding not to sell itself to Microsoft.

Why this decision-making disorder? First, because decisions have generally been viewed as the prerogative of individuals—usually senior executives. The process employed, the information used, the logic relied on, have been left up to them, in something of a black box. Information goes in, decisions come out—and who knows what happens in between? Second, unlike other business processes, decision making has rarely been the focus of systematic analysis inside the firm. Very few organizations have "reengineered" their decisions. Yet there are just as many opportunities to improve decision making as to improve any other process.

Selected Reading

Blink
by Malcolm Gladwell, is a paean to intuitive decision making.

The Wisdom of Crowds
by James Surowiecki, argues for large-group participation in decisions.

How We Decide
by Jonah Lehrer, addresses the psychobiology of decision making and the limits of rationality.

Predictably Irrational
by Dan Ariely, considers behavioral economics and its implications for decision making.

Nudge
by Richard Thaler and Cass Sunstein, is influencing discussions about behavior-oriented policy in Washington, DC.

Two books on analytical and automated decision making:

Competing on Analytics
by Thomas H. Davenport and Jeanne G. Harris

Super Crunchers
by Ian Ayres

Useful insights have been available for a long time. For example, academics defined "groupthink," the forced manufacture of consent, more than half a century ago—yet it still bedevils decision makers from the White House to company boardrooms. In the sixteenth century the Catholic Church established the devil's advocate to criticize canonization decisions—yet few organizations today formalize the advocacy of decision alternatives. Recent popular business books address a host of decision-making alternatives (see "Selected Reading").

However, although businesspeople are clearly buying and reading these books, few companies have actually adopted their recommendations. The consequences of this inattention are becoming

Idea in Brief

Traditionally, decision making in organizations has rarely been the focus of systematic analysis. That may account for the astounding number of recent poor calls, such as decisions to invest in and securitize subprime mortgage loans or to hedge risk with credit default swaps. Business books are rich with insights about the decision process, but organizations have been slow to adopt their recommendations. It's time to focus on decision making, Davenport says, and he proposes four steps: (1) List and prioritize the decisions that must be made; (2) assess the factors that go into each, such as who plays what role, how often the decision must be made, and what information is available to support it; (3) design the roles, processes, systems, and

behaviors your organization needs; and (4) institutionalize decision tools and assistance. The Educational Testing Service and The Stanley Works, among others, have succeeded in improving their decisions. ETS established a centralized deliberative body to make evidence-based decisions about new-product offerings, and Stanley has a Pricing Center of Excellence with internal consultants dedicated to its various business units. Leaders should bring multiple perspectives to their decision making, beware of analytical models that managers don't understand, be clear about their assumptions, practice "model management," and—because only people can revise decision criteria over time—cultivate human backups.

ever more severe. It is time to take decision making out of the realm of the purely individual and idiosyncratic; organizations must help their managers employ better decision-making processes. Better processes won't guarantee better decisions, of course, but they can make them more likely.

A Framework for Improving Decisions

Focusing on decisions doesn't necessarily require a strict focus on the mental processes of managers. (Though, admittedly, the black box deserves some unpacking.) It can mean examining the accessible components of decision making—which decisions need to be made, what information is supplied, key roles in the process, and so forth. Smart organizations make multifaceted interventions—addressing technology, information, organizational structure, methods, and personnel. They can improve decision making in four steps:

1. Identification

Managers should begin by listing the decisions that must be made and deciding which are most important—for example, "the top 10 decisions required to execute our strategy" or "the top 10 decisions that have to go well if we are to meet our financial goals." Some decisions will be rare and highly strategic ("What acquisitions will allow us to gain the necessary market share?") while others will be frequent and on the front lines ("How should we decide how much to pay on claims?"). Without some prioritization, all decisions will be treated as equal—which probably means that the important ones won't be analyzed with sufficient care.

2. Inventory

In addition to identifying key decisions, you should assess the factors that go into each of them. Who plays what role in the decision? How often does it occur? What information is available to support it? How well is the decision typically made? Such an examination helps an organization understand which decisions need improvement and what processes might make them more effective, while establishing a common language for discussing decision making.

3. Intervention

Having narrowed down your list of decisions and examined what's involved in making each, you can design the roles, processes, systems, and behaviors your organization should be using to make them. The key to effective decision interventions is a broad, inclusive approach that considers all methods of improvement and addresses all aspects of the decision process—including execution of the decision, which is often overlooked.

4. Institutionalization

Organizations need to give managers the tools and assistance to "decide how to decide" on an ongoing basis. At Air Products and

Chemicals, for example, managers are trained to determine whether a particular decision should be made unilaterally by one manager, unilaterally after consultation with a group, by a group through a majority vote, or by group consensus. In addition, they determine who will be responsible for making the decision, who will be held accountable for results, and who needs to be consulted or informed.

Companies that are serious about institutionalizing better decision making often enlist decision experts to work with executives on improving the process. Chevron, for example, has a decision-analysis group whose members facilitate decision-framing workshops; coordinate data gathering for analysis; build and refine economic and analytical models; help project managers and decision makers interpret analyses; point out when additional information and analysis would improve a decision; conduct an assessment of decision quality; and coach decision makers. The group has trained more than 2,500 decision makers in two-day workshops and has certified 10,000 through an online training module. At Chevron all major capital projects (which are common at large oil companies) have the benefit of systematic decision analysis.

An organization that has adopted these four steps should also assess the quality of decisions after the fact. The assessment should address not only actual business results—which can involve both politics and luck—but also the decision-making process and whatever information the manager relied on. Chevron regularly performs "lookbacks" on major decisions, and assesses not only outcomes but also how the decision might have employed a better process or addressed uncertainty better.

Let's look at how two companies have improved their decision making.

Better New-Product Decisions at ETS

The Educational Testing Service develops and administers such widely recognized tests as the SAT, the GRE, the TOEFL, and the AP. In 2007 Kurt Landgraf, ETS's CEO, concluded that the organization needed to accelerate and improve decisions about new products and services if it was to continue competing effectively. ETS had previously employed a stage-gate approval process for new offerings, but the organization's matrixed structure and diffuse decision-making responsibility made the process ineffective.

Landgraf asked T.J. Elliott, ETS's vice president of strategic workforce solutions, and Marisa Farnum, the associate vice president for technology transfer, to lead a team that would examine the decision process. The team found several fundamental problems. First, decision makers often lacked information about the intellectual property, partners, cycle times, and likely market for new offerings. Second, it was unclear who played what roles when a decision was being made. Third, the structure of the process was vague.

Elliott and Farnum's team created a new process intended to lead to more evidence-based decisions. It introduced a centralized deliberative body to make decisions about new offerings, developed forms that required new metrics for and information about each proposal, and established standards for what constituted strong evidence that the offering fit with ETS strategy and likely market demand. The process has been in operation for 20 months and is widely regarded as a major improvement. It has clearly resulted in fewer bad product-launch decisions. However, the deliberative body has realized that proposals must be nurtured from an earlier stage to create more good offerings. The scope of its governance was expanded recently to evaluate and prioritize all product-adaptation and new-product opportunities.

Better Pricing Decisions at The Stanley Works

The Stanley Works, a maker of tools and other products for construction, industry, and security, has been operating its Pricing Center of Excellence since 2003. Under the banner of the Stanley Fulfillment System, a broad initiative for continual improvement in operations, Stanley had identified several decision domains that were critical to its success, including pricing, sales and operational planning, fulfillment processes, and lean manufacturing. Because all of them had a strong information component, a center of excellence was formed for each. The pricing center brings deep knowledge of pricing, data and analysis tools, and relationships with pricing experts at consulting and software firms to Stanley's business units. It is staffed by a director, internal consultants dedicated to the business units, and IT and data-mining specialists.

The center has made a variety of interventions in how the business units reach and execute pricing decisions. Over time it has developed several pricing methodologies and is now focusing on pricing optimization approaches. It has recommended assigning pricing responsibilities to the business unit managers. It holds regular "gross margin calls" with the units to share successes and review failures. (Stanley's CEO, John Lundgren, and its COO, Jim Loree, frequently participate.) Pricing outcomes have been added to personnel evaluations and compensation reviews. An offshore supplier has been engaged to gather and analyze competitors' prices. The center has helped to develop automated decision making, such as a process for authorizing promotional events. It uses "white space analysis" to analyze customer sales data and identify opportunities for additional sales or margin. It also trains the business units on pricing methods, participates in project start-ups, does coaching and mentoring, and disseminates innovations and best practices in pricing.

The results of the center's work speak for themselves: Gross margin at Stanley grew from 33.9% to more than 40% in six years. The changes have delivered more than $200 million in incremental value to the firm. Bert Davis, Stanley's head of business transformation and information systems, says, "We tried to improve pricing decisions with data and analysis tools alone, but it didn't work. It was only when we established the center that we began to see real improvement in pricing decisions."

Multiple Perspectives Yield Better Results

Analytics and decision automation are among the most powerful tools for improving decision making. A growing number of firms are embracing the former both strategically and tactically, building competitive strategies around their analytical capabilities and making decisions on the basis of data and analytics. (See my article "Competing on Analytics," HBR January 2006.) Analytics are even more effective when they have been embedded in automated systems, which can make many decisions virtually in real time. (Few mortgages or insurance policies in the United States are drawn up without decision automation.)

But if one of these approaches goes awry, it can do serious damage to your business. If you're making poor decisions on loans or insurance policies with an automated system, for example, you can lose money in a torrent—just ask those bankers who issued so many low-quality subprime loans. Therefore, it's critical to balance and augment these decision tools with human intuition and judgment. Organizations should:

- Warn managers not to build into their businesses analytical models they don't understand. This means, of course, that to be effective, managers must increasingly be numerate with analytics. As the Yale economist Robert Shiller told the *McKinsey Quarterly* in April 2009, "You have to be a quantitative person if you're managing a company. The quantitative details really matter."

- Make assumptions clear. Every model has assumptions behind it, such as "Housing prices will continue to rise for the foreseeable future" or "Loan charge-off levels will remain similar to those of the past 10 years." (Both these assumptions, of course, have recently been discredited.) Knowing what the assumptions are makes it possible to anticipate when models are no longer a guide to effective decisions.

- Practice "model management," which keeps track of the models being used within an organization and monitors how well they are working to analyze and predict selected variables. Capital One, an early adopter, has many analytical models in place to support marketing and operations.

The new landscape of decision making

Ancient approaches to decision making have recently been augmented by improvements in technology and new research. But every approach has both benefits and drawbacks.

	Small-group process	Analytics	Automation	Neuroscience
Benefits	premature convergence on decisions is unlikely	decisions are more likely to be correct	speed and accuracy	decision makers know when to use the emotional brain
	clear responsibilities can be assigned	the scientific method adds rigor	criteria for decisions are clear	trains the rational brain to perform more effectively
	multiple alternatives can be examined			individual decision making may be overvalued
Cautionary messages	norms for debate must be rational, not emotional	gathering enough data may be difficult and time-consuming	difficult to develop	the brain is still poorly understood
	everyone must get on board with the decision after debate	correct assumptions are crucial	decision criteria may change	

(continued)

	Behavioral economics	Intuition	Wisdom of crowds
Benefits	incorporating research on economic behavior and thinking into decisions	relying on one's gut and experience to make decisions	using surveys or markets to allow decisions or inputs by large groups
Cautionary messages	illuminates biases and areas of irrationality	easy and requires no data	those close to the issue are well positioned to know the truth
	can nudge decisions in a particular direction	the subconscious can be effective at weighing options	crowd-based decisions can be very accurate
	findings in the field are still sketchy	typically the least accurate of decision approaches	members of the crowd must not influence one another
	context and wording can be used to manipulate decisions	decision makers are easily swayed by context	ongoing participation is difficult to maintain

- Cultivate human backups. Automated decision systems are often used to replace human decision makers—but you lose those people at your peril. It takes an expert human being to revise decision criteria over time or know when an automated algorithm no longer works well.

It's also important to know when a particular decision approach doesn't apply. For example, analytics isn't a good fit in situations when you have to make a really fast decision. And almost all quantitative models—even predictive ones—are based on past data, so if your experience or intuition tells you that the past is no longer a good guide to the present and future, you'll want to employ other decision tools, or at least to create some new data and analyses. (For a quick look at the strengths and weaknesses of various approaches, see the exhibit "The new landscape of decision making.")

Decisions, like any other business activity, won't get better without systematic review. If you don't know which of your decisions are most important, you won't be able to prioritize improvements. If you don't know how decisions are made in your company, you can't change the process for making them. If you don't assess the results of your changes, you're unlikely to achieve better decisions. The way to begin is simply to give decisions the attention they deserve. Without it, any success your organization achieves in decision making will be largely a matter of luck.

Originally published in November 2009. Reprint R0911L

Why Good Leaders Make Bad Decisions

by Andrew Campbell, Jo Whitehead, and Sydney Finkelstein

DECISION MAKING LIES AT THE heart of our personal and professional lives. Every day we make decisions. Some are small, domestic, and innocuous. Others are more important, affecting people's lives, livelihoods, and well-being. Inevitably, we make mistakes along the way. The daunting reality is that enormously important decisions made by intelligent, responsible people with the best information and intentions are sometimes hopelessly flawed.

Consider Jürgen Schrempp, CEO of Daimler-Benz. He led the merger of Chrysler and Daimler against internal opposition. Nine years later, Daimler was forced to virtually give Chrysler away in a private equity deal. Steve Russell, chief executive of Boots, the UK drugstore chain, launched a health care strategy designed to differentiate the stores from competitors and grow through new health care services such as dentistry. It turned out, though, that Boots managers did not have the skills needed to succeed in health care services, and many of these markets offered little profit potential. The strategy contributed to Russell's early departure from the top job. Brigadier General Matthew Broderick, chief of the Homeland Security Operations Center, who was responsible for alerting President Bush and other senior government officials if Hurricane Katrina breached the levees in New Orleans, went home on Monday,

August 29, 2005, after reporting that they seemed to be holding, despite multiple reports of breaches.

All these executives were highly qualified for their jobs, and yet they made decisions that soon seemed clearly wrong. Why? And more important, how can we avoid making similar mistakes? This is the topic we've been exploring for the past four years, and the journey has taken us deep into a field called decision neuroscience. We began by assembling a database of 83 decisions that we felt were flawed at the time they were made. From our analysis of these cases, we concluded that flawed decisions start with errors of judgment made by influential individuals. Hence we needed to understand how these errors of judgment occur.

In the following pages, we will describe the conditions that promote errors of judgment and explore ways organizations can build protections into the decision-making process to reduce the risk of mistakes. We'll conclude by showing how two leading companies applied the approach we describe. To put all this in context, however, we first need to understand just how the human brain forms its judgments.

How the Brain Trips Up

We depend primarily on two hardwired processes for decision making. Our brains assess what's going on using pattern recognition, and we react to that information—or ignore it—because of emotional tags that are stored in our memories. Both of these processes are normally reliable; they are part of our evolutionary advantage. But in certain circumstances, both can let us down.

Pattern recognition is a complex process that integrates information from as many as 30 different parts of the brain. Faced with a new situation, we make assumptions based on prior experiences and judgments. Thus a chess master can assess a chess game and choose a high-quality move in as little as six seconds by drawing on patterns he or she has seen before. But pattern recognition can also mislead us. When we're dealing with seemingly familiar situations, our brains can cause us to think we understand them when we don't.

Idea in Brief

Decision making lies at the heart of our personal and professional lives. Yet the daunting reality is that enormously important decisions made by intelligent, responsible people with the best information and intentions are nevertheless hopelessly flawed at times. In part, that's due to the way our brains work. Modern neuroscience teaches us that two hard-wired processes in the brain—pattern recognition and emotional tagging—are critical to decision making. Both are normally reliable; indeed, they provide us with an evolutionary advantage. But in certain circumstances, either one can trip us up and skew our judgment. In this article, Campbell and Whitehead, directors at the Ashridge Strategic Management Centre, together with Finkelstein, of Dartmouth's Tuck School, describe the conditions that promote errors of judgment and explore how organizations can build safeguards against them into the decision-making process. In their analysis, the authors delineate three "red-flag conditions" that are responsible either for distorting emotional tagging or for encouraging people to see false patterns: conflicts of interest; attachments to people, places, or things; and the presence of misleading memories, which seem, but really are not, relevant and comparable to the current situation. Using a global chemical company as an example, the authors describe the steps leaders can take to counteract those biases: inject fresh experience or analysis, introduce further debate and more challenges to their thinking, and impose stronger governance. Rather than rely on the wisdom of experienced chairmen, the humility of CEOs, or the standard organizational checks and balances, the authors urge, everyone involved in important decisions should explicitly consider whether red flags exist and, if they do, lobby for appropriate safeguards.

What happened to Matthew Broderick during Hurricane Katrina is instructive. Broderick had been involved in operations centers in Vietnam and in other military engagements, and he had led the Homeland Security Operations Center during previous hurricanes. These experiences had taught him that early reports surrounding a major event are often false: It's better to wait for the "ground truth" from a reliable source before acting. Unfortunately, he had no experience with a hurricane hitting a city built below sea level.

By late on August 29, some 12 hours after Katrina hit New Orleans, Broderick had received 17 reports of major flooding and levee breaches. But he also had gotten conflicting information. The Army Corps of Engineers had reported that it had no evidence of levee breaches, and a late afternoon CNN report from Bourbon Street in the French Quarter had shown city dwellers partying and claiming they had dodged the bullet. Broderick's pattern-recognition process told him that these contrary reports were the ground truth he was looking for. So before going home for the night, he issued a situation report stating that the levees had not been breached, although he did add that further assessment would be needed the next day.

Emotional tagging is the process by which emotional information attaches itself to the thoughts and experiences stored in our memories. This emotional information tells us whether to pay attention to something or not, and it tells us what sort of action we should be contemplating (immediate or postponed, fight or flight). When the parts of our brains controlling emotions are damaged, we can see how important emotional tagging is: Neurological research shows that we become slow and incompetent decision makers even though we can retain the capacity for objective analysis.

Like pattern recognition, emotional tagging helps us reach sensible decisions most of the time. But it, too, can mislead us. Take the case of Wang Laboratories, the top company in the word-processing industry in the early 1980s. Recognizing that his company's future was threatened by the rise of the personal computer, founder An Wang built a machine to compete in this sector. Unfortunately, he chose to create a proprietary operating system despite the fact that the IBM PC was clearly becoming the dominant standard in the industry. This blunder, which contributed to Wang's demise a few years later, was heavily influenced by An Wang's dislike of IBM. He believed he had been cheated by IBM over a new technology he had invented early in his career. These feelings made him reject a software platform linked to an IBM product even though the platform was provided by a third party, Microsoft.

Why doesn't the brain pick up on such errors and correct them? The most obvious reason is that much of the mental work we do is unconscious. This makes it hard to check the data and logic we use when we make a decision. Typically, we spot bugs in our personal software only when we see the results of our errors in judgment. Matthew Broderick found out that his ground-truth rule of thumb was an inappropriate response to Hurricane Katrina only after it was too late. An Wang found out that his preference for proprietary software was flawed only after Wang's personal computer failed in the market.

Compounding the problem of high levels of unconscious thinking is the lack of checks and balances in our decision making. Our brains do not naturally follow the classical textbook model: Lay out the options, define the objectives, and assess each option against each objective. Instead, we analyze the situation using pattern recognition and arrive at a decision to act or not by using emotional tags. The two processes happen almost instantaneously. Indeed, as the research of psychologist Gary Klein shows, our brains leap to conclusions and are reluctant to consider alternatives. Moreover, we are particularly bad at revisiting our initial assessment of a situation—our initial frame.

An exercise we frequently run at Ashridge Business School shows how hard it is to challenge the initial frame. We give students a case that presents a new technology as a good business opportunity. Often, a team works many hours before it challenges this frame and starts, correctly, to see the new technology as a major threat to the company's dominant market position. Even though the financial model consistently calculates negative returns from launching the new technology, some teams never challenge their original frame and end up proposing aggressive investments.

Raising the Red Flag

In analyzing how it is that good leaders made bad judgments, we found they were affected in all cases by three factors that either distorted their emotional tags or encouraged them to see a false pattern. We call these factors "red flag conditions."

The first and most familiar red flag condition, *the presence of inappropriate self-interest,* typically biases the emotional importance we place on information, which in turn makes us readier to perceive the patterns we want to see. Research has shown that even well-intentioned professionals, such as doctors and auditors, are unable to prevent self-interest from biasing their judgments of which medicine to prescribe or opinion to give during an audit.

The second, somewhat less familiar condition is *the presence of distorting attachments*. We can become attached to people, places, and things, and these bonds can affect the judgments we form about both the situation we face and the appropriate actions to take. The reluctance executives often feel to sell a unit they've worked in nicely captures the power of inappropriate attachments.

The final red flag condition is *the presence of misleading memories*. These are memories that seem relevant and comparable to the current situation but lead our thinking down the wrong path. They can cause us to overlook or undervalue some important differentiating factors, as Matthew Broderick did when he gave too little thought to the implications of a hurricane hitting a city below sea level. The chance of being misled by memories is intensified by any emotional tags we have attached to the past experience. If our decisions in the previous similar experience worked well, we'll be all the more likely to overlook key differences.

That's what happened to William Smithburg, former chairman of Quaker Oats. He acquired Snapple because of his vivid memories of Gatorade, Quaker's most successful deal. Snapple, like Gatorade, appeared to be a new drinks company that could be improved with Quaker's marketing and management skills. Unfortunately, the similarities between Snapple and Gatorade proved to be superficial, which meant that Quaker ended up destroying rather than creating value. In fact, Snapple was Smithburg's worst deal.

Of course, part of what we are saying is common knowledge: People have biases, and it's important to manage decisions so that these biases balance out. Many experienced leaders do this already. But we're arguing here that, given the way the brain works, we cannot rely on leaders to spot and safeguard against their own errors in judgment. For important decisions, we need a deliberate, structured way to identify likely sources of bias—those red flag conditions—and we need to strengthen the group decision-making process.

Consider the situation faced by Rita Chakra, head of the cosmetics business of Choudry Holdings (the names of the companies and people cited in this and the following examples have been disguised). She was promoted head of the consumer products division and needed to decide whether to promote her number two into her cosmetics job or recruit someone from outside. Can we anticipate any potential red flags in this decision? Yes, her emotional tags could be unreliable because of a distorting attachment she may have to her colleague or an inappropriate self-interest she could have in keeping her workload down while changing jobs. Of course we don't know for certain whether Rita feels this attachment or holds that vested interest. And since the greater part of decision making is unconscious, Rita would not know either. What we do know is that there is a risk. So how should Rita protect herself, or how should her boss help her protect herself?

The simple answer is to involve someone else—someone who has no inappropriate attachments or self-interest. This could be Rita's boss, the head of human resources, a headhunter, or a trusted colleague. That person could challenge her thinking, force her to review her logic, encourage her to consider options, and possibly even champion a solution she would find uncomfortable. Fortunately, in this situation, Rita was already aware of some red flag conditions, and so she involved a headhunter to help her evaluate her colleague and external candidates. In the end, Rita did appoint her colleague but only after checking to see if her judgment was biased.

We've found many leaders who intuitively understand that their thinking or their colleagues' thinking can be distorted. But few leaders do so in a structured way, and as a result many fail to provide sufficient safeguards against bad decisions. Let's look now at a couple of companies that approached the problem of decision bias systematically by recognizing and reducing the risk posed by red flag conditions.

Safeguarding Against Your Biases

A European multinational we'll call Global Chemicals had an underperforming division. The management team in charge of the division had twice promised a turnaround and twice failed to deliver. The CEO, Mark Thaysen, was weighing his options.

This division was part of Thaysen's growth strategy. It had been assembled over the previous five years through two large and four smaller acquisitions. Thaysen had led the two larger acquisitions and appointed the managers who were struggling to perform. The chairman of the supervisory board, Olaf Grunweld, decided to consider whether Thaysen's judgment about the underperforming division might be biased and, if so, how he might help. Grunweld was not second-guessing Thaysen's thinking. He was merely alert to the possibility that the CEO's views might be distorted.

Grunweld started by looking for red flag conditions. (For a description of a process for identifying red flags, see the sidebar, "Identifying Red Flags.") Thaysen built the underperforming division, and his attachment to it might have made him reluctant to abandon the strategy or the team he had put in place. What's more, because in the past he had successfully supported the local managers during a tough turnaround in another division, Thaysen ran the risk of seeing the wrong pattern and unconsciously favoring the view that continued support was needed in this situation, too. Thus alerted to Thaysen's possible distorting attachments and potential misleading memories, Grunweld considered three types of safeguards to strengthen the decision process.

Injecting fresh experience or analysis

You can often counteract biases by exposing the decision maker to new information and a different take on the problem. In this instance, Grunweld asked an investment bank to tell Thaysen what value the company might get from selling the underperforming division. Grunweld felt this would encourage Thaysen to at least consider that radical option—a step Thaysen might too quickly dismiss if he had become overly attached to the unit or its management team.

Identifying Red Flags

RED FLAGS ARE USEFUL ONLY if they can be spotted before a decision is made. How can you recognize them in complex situations? We have developed the following seven-step process:

1. **Lay out the range of options.** It's never possible to list them all. But it's normally helpful to note the extremes. These provide boundaries for the decision.

2. **List the main decision makers.** Who is going to be influential in making the judgment calls and the final choice? There may be only one or two people involved. But there could also be 10 or more.

3. **Choose one decision maker to focus on.** It's usually best to start with the most influential person. Then identify red flag conditions that might distort that individual's thinking.

4. **Check for inappropriate self-interest or distorting attachments.** Is any option likely to be particularly attractive or unattractive to the decision maker because of personal interests or attachments to people, places, or things? Do any of these interests or attachments conflict with the objectives of the main stakeholders?

5. **Check for misleading memories.** What are the uncertainties in this decision? For each area of uncertainty, consider whether the decision maker might draw on potentially misleading memories. Think about past experiences that could mislead, especially ones with strong emotional associations. Think also about previous judgments that could now be unsound, given the current situation.

6. **Repeat the analysis with the next most influential person.** In a complex case, it may be necessary to consider many more people, and the process may bring to light a long list of possible red flags.

7. **Review the list of red flags you have identified** and determine whether the brain's normally efficient pattern-recognition and emotional-tagging processes might be biased in favor of or against some options. If so, put one or more safeguards in place.

Introducing further debate and challenge

This safeguard can ensure that biases are confronted explicitly. It works best when the power structure of the group debating the issue is balanced. While Thaysen's chief financial officer was a strong individual, Grunweld felt that the other members of the executive group would be likely to follow Thaysen's lead without challenging him. Moreover, the head of the underperforming division was a member of the executive group, making it hard for open debate to occur. So Grunweld proposed a steering committee consisting of himself, Thaysen, and the CFO. Even if Thaysen strongly pushed for a particular solution, Grunweld and the CFO would make sure his reasoning was properly challenged and debated. Grunweld also suggested that Thaysen set up a small project team, led by the head of strategy, to analyze all the options and present them to the steering committee.

Imposing stronger governance
The requirement that a decision be ratified at a higher level provides a final safeguard. Stronger governance does not eliminate distorted thinking, but it can prevent distortions from leading to a bad outcome. At Global Chemicals, the governance layer was the supervisory board. Grunweld realized, however, that its objectivity could be compromised because he was a member of both the board and the steering committee. So he asked two of his board colleagues to be ready to argue against the proposal emanating from the steering committee if they felt uncomfortable.

In the end, the steering committee proposed an outright sale of the division, a decision the board approved. The price received was well above expectations, convincing all that they had chosen the best option.

The chairman of Global Chemicals took the lead role in designing the decision process. That was appropriate given the importance of the decision. But many decisions are made at the operating level, where direct CEO involvement is neither feasible nor desirable. That was the case at Southern Electricity, a division of a larger U.S. utility. Southern consisted of three operating units and two powerful functions. Recent regulatory changes meant that prices could not be raised and might even fall. So managers were looking for ways to cut back on capital expenditures.

Division head Jack Williams recognized that the managers were also risk averse, preferring to replace equipment early with the best upgrades available. This, he realized, was a result of some high-profile breakdowns in the past, which had exposed individuals both to complaints from customers and to criticism from colleagues. Williams believed the emotional tags associated with these experiences might be distorting their judgment.

What could he do to counteract these effects? Williams rejected the idea of stronger governance; he felt that neither his management team nor the parent company's executives knew enough to do the job credibly. He also rejected additional analysis, because Southern's analysis was already rigorous. He concluded that he had to find a way to inject more debate into the decision process and enable people who understood the details to challenge the thinking.

His first thought was to involve himself and his head of finance in the debates, but he didn't have time to consider the merits of hundreds of projects, and he didn't understand the details well enough to effectively challenge decisions earlier in the process than he currently was doing, at the final approval stage. Williams finally decided to get the unit and function heads to challenge one another, facilitated by a consultant. Rather than impose this process on his managers, Williams chose to share his thinking with them. Using the language of red flags, he was able to get them to see the problem without their feeling threatened. The new approach was very successful. The reduced capital-expenditure target was met with room to spare and without Williams having to make any of the tough judgment calls himself.

Because we now understand more about how the brain works, we can anticipate the circumstances in which errors of judgment may occur and guard against them. So rather than rely on the wisdom of experienced chairmen, the humility of CEOs, or the standard organizational checks and balances, we urge all involved in important decisions to explicitly consider whether red flags exist and, if they do, to lobby for appropriate safeguards. Decisions that involve no red flags need many fewer checks and balances and thus less bureaucracy. Some of those resources could then be devoted to protecting the decisions most at risk with more intrusive and robust protections.

Originally published in February 2009. **Reprint** R0902D

Stop Making Plans; Start Making Decisions

by Michael C. Mankins and Richard Steele

IS STRATEGIC PLANNING COMPLETELY USELESS? That was the question the CEO of a global manufacturer recently asked himself. Two years earlier, he had launched an ambitious overhaul of the company's planning process. The old approach, which required business-unit heads to make regular presentations to the firm's executive committee, had broken down entirely. The ExCom members—the CEO, COO, CFO, CTO, and head of HR—had grown tired of sitting through endless PowerPoint presentations that provided them few opportunities to challenge the business units' assumptions or influence their strategies. And the unit heads had complained that the ExCom reviews were long on exhortation but short on executable advice. Worse, the reviews led to very few worthwhile decisions.

The revamped process incorporated state-of-the-art thinking about strategic planning. To avoid information overload, it limited each business to 15 "high-impact" exhibits describing the unit's strategy. To ensure thoughtful discussions, it required that all presentations and supporting materials be distributed to the ExCom at least a week in advance. The review sessions themselves were restructured to allow ample time for give-and-take between the corporate team and the business-unit executives. And rather than force the unit heads to traipse off to headquarters for meetings, the ExCom agreed to spend an unprecedented six weeks each spring visiting all 22 units for daylong sessions. The intent was to make the strategy reviews longer, more focused, and more consequential.

It didn't work. After using the new process for two planning cycles, the CEO gathered feedback from the participants through an anonymous survey. To his dismay, the report contained a litany of complaints: "It takes too much time." "It's at too high a level." "It's disconnected from the way we run the business." And so on. Most damning of all, however, was the respondents' near-universal view that the new approach produced very few real decisions. The CEO was dumbfounded. How could the company's cutting-edge planning process still be so badly broken? More important, what should he do to make strategic planning drive more, better, and faster decisions?

Like this CEO, many executives have grown skeptical of strategic planning. Is it any wonder? Despite all the time and energy most companies put into strategic planning, the process is most often a barrier to good decision making, our research indicates. As a result, strategic planning doesn't really influence most companies' strategy.

In the following pages, we will demonstrate that the failure of most strategic planning is due to two factors: It is typically an annual process, and it is most often focused on individual business units. As such, the process is completely at odds with the way executives actually make important strategy decisions, which are neither constrained by the calendar nor defined by unit boundaries. Not surprisingly, then, senior executives routinely sidestep the planning process. They make the decisions that really shape their company's strategy and determine its future—decisions about mergers and acquisitions, product launches, corporate restructurings, and the like—outside the planning process, typically in an ad hoc fashion, without rigorous analysis or productive debate. Critical decisions are made incorrectly or not at all. More than anything else, this disconnect—between the way planning works and the way decision

Idea in Brief

Most executives view traditional strategic planning as worthless. Why? The process contains serious flaws. First, it's conducted annually, so it doesn't help executives respond swiftly to threats and opportunities (a new competitor, a possible acquisition) that crop up throughout the year.

Second, it unfolds unit by unit—with executive committee members visiting one unit at a time to review their strategic plans. Executives lack sufficient information to provide worthwhile guidance during these "business tours." And the visits take them away from urgent companywide issues, such as whether to enter a new market, outsource a function, or restructure the organization.

Frustrated by these constraints, executives routinely sidestep their company's formal strategic planning process—making ad hoc decisions based on scanty analysis and meager debate. Result? Decisions made incorrectly, too slowly, or not at all.

How to improve the quality *and* quantity of your strategic decisions? Use **continuous issues-focused strategic planning**. Throughout the year, identify the issues you must resolve to enhance your company's performance—particularly those spanning multiple business units. Debate one issue at a time until you've reached a decision. And add issues to your agenda as business realities change.

Your reward? More rigorous debate and more significant strategic decisions each year—made precisely when they're needed.

making happens—explains the frustration, if not outright antipathy, most executives feel toward strategic planning.

But companies can fix the process if they attack its root problems. A small number of forward-looking companies have thrown out their calendar-driven, business-unit-focused planning processes and replaced them with continuous, issues-focused decision making. By changing the timing and focus of strategic planning, they've also changed the nature of top management's discussions about strategy—from "review and approve" to "debate and decide," meaning that senior executives seriously think through every major decision and its implications for the company's performance and value. Indeed, these companies use the strategy development process to drive decision making. As a consequence, they make more

Idea in Practice

To create an effective strategic-planning process:

Link Decision Making and Planning. Create a mechanism that helps you identify the decisions you *must* make to create more shareholder value. Once you've made those decisions, use your traditional planning process to develop an implementation road map.

> *Example:* At Boeing Commercial Airplanes, executives meet regularly to uncover the company's most pressing, long-term strategic issues (such as evolving product strategy, or fueling growth in services). Upon selecting a course of action, they update their long-range business plan with an implementation strategy for that decision. (By separating—but linking—planning and execution, Boeing

makes faster and better decisions.)

Focus on Companywide Issues. During strategy discussions, focus on issues spanning multiple business units.

> *Example:* Facing a shortage of investment ideas, Microsoft's leaders began defining issues—such as PC market growth and security—that are critical throughout the company. Dialogues between unit leaders and the executive committee now focus on what Microsoft as a whole can do to address each issue—not which strategies individual units should formulate. Countless new growth opportunities have surfaced.

Develop Strategy Continuously. Spread strategy reviews throughout the year rather than squeezing

than twice as many important strategic decisions each year as companies that follow the traditional planning model. (See the sidebar "Who Makes More Decisions?") These companies have stopped making plans and started making decisions.

Where Planning Goes Wrong

In the fall of 2005, Marakon Associates, in collaboration with the Economist Intelligence Unit, surveyed senior executives from 156 large companies worldwide, all with sales of $1 billion or more (40% of them had revenues over $10 billion). We asked these executives how their companies developed long-range plans and how them into a two- or three-month window. You'll be able to focus on—and resolve—one issue at a time. And you'll have the flexibility to add issues as soon as business conditions change.

Example: Executives at multi-industry giant Textron review two to three units' strategy per quarter rather than compressing all unit reviews into one quarter annually. They also hold continuous reviews designed to address each strategic issue on the company's agenda. Once an also-ran among its peers, Textron was a top-quartile performer during 2004–2005.

Structure Strategy Reviews to Produce Results. Design and conduct strategy sessions so that participants agree on facts related to each issue before proposing solutions.

Example: At Textron, each strategic issue is resolved through a disciplined process: In one session, the management committee debates the issue at hand and reaches agreement on the relevant facts (e.g., customers' purchase behaviors, a key market's profitability figures). The group then generates several viable strategy alternatives. In a second session, the committee evaluates the alternatives from a strategic and financial perspective and selects a course of action. By moving from facts to alternatives to choices, the group reaches many more decisions than before.

effectively they thought their planning processes drove strategic decisions.

The results of the survey confirmed what we have observed over many years of consulting: The timing and structure of strategic planning are obstacles to good decision making. Specifically, we found that companies with standard planning processes and practices make only 2.5 major strategic decisions each year, on average (by "major," we mean they have the potential to increase company profits by 10% or more over the long term). It's hard to imagine that with so few strategic decisions driving growth, these companies can keep moving forward and deliver the financial performance that investors expect.

Who Makes More Decisions?

COMPANIES SEE A DRAMATIC INCREASE in the quality of their decision making once they abandon the traditional planning model, which is calendar driven and focused on the business units. In our survey, the companies that broke most completely with the past made more than twice as many strategic decisions each year as companies wedded to tradition. What's more, the new structure of the planning process ensures that the decisions are probably the best that could have been made, given the information available to managers at the time.

Here are the average numbers of major strategic decisions reached per year in companies that take the following approaches to strategic planning:

Annual review focused on business units

2.5 decisions per year

Annual review focused on issues

3.5 decisions per year

Continuous review focused on business units

4.1 decisions per year

Continuous review focused on issues

6.1 decisions per year

Source: Marakon Associates and the Economist Intelligence Unit

Even worse, we suspect that the few decisions companies do reach are made in spite of the strategic planning process, not because of it. Indeed, the traditional planning model is so cumbersome and out of sync with the way executives want and need to make decisions that top managers all too often sidestep the process when making their biggest strategic choices.

With the big decisions being made outside the planning process, strategic planning becomes merely a codification of judgments top management has already made, rather than a vehicle for identifying and debating the critical decisions that the company needs to make to produce superior performance. Over time, managers begin to question the value of strategic planning, withdraw from it, and come to rely on other processes for setting company strategy.

The calendar effect

At 66% of the companies in our survey, planning is a periodic event, often conducted as a precursor to the yearly budgeting and capital-approval processes. In fact, linking strategic planning to these other management processes is often cited as a best practice. But forcing strategic planning into an annual cycle risks making it irrelevant to executives, who must make many important decisions throughout the year.

There are two major drawbacks to such a rigid schedule. The first might be called the *time* problem. A once-a-year planning schedule simply does not give executives sufficient time to address the issues that most affect performance. According to our survey, companies that follow an annual planning calendar devote less than nine weeks per year to strategy development. That's barely two months to collect relevant facts, set strategic priorities, weigh competing alternatives, and make important strategic choices. Many issues—particularly those spanning multiple businesses, crossing geographic boundaries, or involving entire value chains—cannot be resolved effectively in such a short time. It took Boeing, for example, almost two years to decide to outsource major activities such as wing manufacturing.

Constrained by the planning calendar, corporate executives face two choices: They can either not address these complex issues—in effect, throwing them in the "too-hard" bucket—or they can address them through some process other than strategic planning. In both cases, strategic planning is marginalized and separated from strategic decision making.

Then there's the *timing* problem. Even when executives allot sufficient time in strategy development to address tough issues, the timing of the process can create problems. At most companies, strategic planning is a batch process in which managers analyze market and competitor information, identify threats and opportunities, and then define a multiyear plan. But in the real world, managers make strategic decisions continuously, often motivated by an immediate need for action (or reaction). When a new competitor enters a market, for instance, or a rival introduces a new technology, executives must act quickly and decisively to safeguard the company's performance. But very few companies (less than 10%, according to our survey) have any sort of rigorous or disciplined process for responding to changes in the external environment. Instead, managers rely on ad hoc processes to correct course or make opportunistic moves. Once again, strategic planning is sidelined, and executives risk making poor decisions that have not been carefully thought through.

M&A decisions provide a particularly egregious example of the timing problem. Acquisition opportunities tend to emerge spontaneously, the result of changes in management at a target company, the actions of a competitor, or some other unpredictable event. Faced with a promising opportunity and limited time in which to act, executives can't wait until the opportunity is evaluated as part of the next annual planning cycle, so they assess the deal and make a quick decision. But because there's often no proper review process, the softer customer- and people-related issues so critical to effective integration of an acquired company can get shortchanged. It is no coincidence that failure to plan for integration is often cited as the primary cause of deal failure.

The business-unit effect

The organizational focus of the typical planning process compounds its calendar effects—or, perhaps more aptly, defects. Two-thirds of the executives we surveyed indicated that strategic planning at their companies is conducted business by business—that is, it is focused on units or groups of units. But 70% of the senior executives who responded to our survey stated they make decisions issue by issue. For example, should we enter China? Should we outsource manufacturing? Should we acquire our distributor? Given this mismatch between the way planning is organized and the way big decisions are made, it's hardly surprising that, once again, corporate leaders look elsewhere for guidance and inspiration. In fact, only 11% of the executives we surveyed believed strongly that planning was worth the effort.

The organizational focus of traditional strategic planning also creates distance, even antagonism, between corporate executives

Traditional Planning

COMPANIES THAT FOLLOW THE TRADITIONAL strategic planning model develop a strategy plan for each business unit at some point during the year. A cross-functional team dedicates less than nine weeks to developing the unit's plan. The executive committee reviews each plan—typically in daylong, on-site meetings—and rubber-stamps the results. The plans are consolidated to produce a companywide strategic plan for review by the board of directors.

Once the strategic-planning cycle is complete, the units dedicate another eight to nine weeks to budgeting and capital planning (in most companies, these processes are not explicitly linked to strategic planning).

The executive committee then holds another round of meetings with each of the business units to negotiate performance targets, resource commitments, and (in many cases) compensation for managers.

The results: an approved but potentially unrealistic strategic plan for each business unit and a separate budget for each unit that is decoupled from the unit's strategic plan.

and business-unit managers. Consider, for example, the way most companies conduct strategy reviews—as formal meetings between senior managers and the heads of each business unit. While these reviews are intended to produce a fact-based dialogue, they often amount to little more than business tourism. The executive committee flies in for a day, sees the sights, meets the natives, and flies out. The business unit, for its part, puts in a lot of work preparing for this royal visit and is keen to make it smooth and trouble free. The unit hopes to escape with few unanswered questions and an approved plan. Accordingly, local managers control the flow of information upward, and senior managers are presented only with information that shows each unit in the best possible light. Opportunities are highlighted; threats are downplayed or omitted.

Even if there's no subterfuge, senior corporate managers still have trouble engaging in constructive dialogue and debate because of what might be called information asymmetry. They just don't have the information they need to be helpful in guiding business units. So when they're presented with a strategic plan that's too good to be believed, they have only two real options: either reject

Continuous, Decision-Oriented Planning

ONCE THE COMPANY AS A whole has identified its most important strategic priorities (typically in an annual strategy update), executive committee dialogues, spread throughout the year, are set up to reach decisions on as many issues as possible. Since issues frequently span multiple business units, task forces are established to prepare the strategic and financial information that's needed to uncover and evaluate strategy alternatives for each issue. Preparation time may exceed nine weeks. The executive committee engages in two dialogues for each issue at three to four hours each. The first dialogue focuses on reaching agreement on the facts surrounding the issue and on a set of viable alternatives. The second focuses on the evaluation of those alternatives and the selection of the best course of action. Once an issue is resolved, a new one is added to the agenda. Critical issues can be inserted into the planning process at any time as market and competitive conditions change.

Once a decision has been reached, the budgets and capital plans for the affected business units are updated to reflect the selected option. Consequently, the strategic-planning process and the capital and budgeting processes are integrated. This significantly reduces the need for lengthy negotiations between the executive committee and unit management over the budget and capital plan.

it—a move that's all but unheard-of at most large companies—or play along and impose stretch targets to secure at least the promise that the unit will improve performance. In both cases, the review does little to drive decisions on issues. It's hardly surprising that only 13% of the executives we surveyed felt that top managers were effectively engaged in all aspects of strategy development at their companies—from target setting to debating alternatives to approving strategies and allocating resources.

Decision-Focused Strategic Planning

Strategic planning can't have impact if it doesn't drive decision making. And it can't drive decision making as long as it remains focused on individual business units and limited by the calendar. Over the past several years, we have observed that many of the best-performing companies have abandoned the traditional approach

The results: a concrete plan for addressing each key issue; for each business unit, a continuously updated budget and capital plan that is linked directly to the resolution of critical strategic issues; and more, faster, better decisions per year.

and are focusing explicitly on reaching decisions through the continuous identification and systematic resolution of strategic issues. (The sidebar "Continuous, Decision-Oriented Planning" presents a detailed example of the issues-oriented approach.) Although these companies have found different specific solutions, all have made essentially the same fundamental changes to their planning and strategy development processes in order to produce more, better, and faster decisions.

They separate—but integrate—decision making and plan making
First and most important, a company must take decisions out of the traditional planning process and create a different, parallel process for developing strategy that helps executives identify the decisions they *need to make* to create more shareholder value over time. The output of this new process isn't a plan at all—it's a set of concrete decisions that management can codify into future business plans through the

existing planning process, which remains in place. Identifying and making decisions is distinct from creating, monitoring, and updating a strategic plan, and the two sets of tasks require very different, but integrated, processes.

Boeing Commercial Airplanes (BCA) is a case in point. This business unit, Boeing's largest, has had a long-range business plan (LRBP) process for many years. The protracted cycles of commercial aircraft production require the unit's CEO, Alan Mulally, and his leadership team to take a long-term view of the business. Accordingly, the unit's LRBP contains a ten-year financial forecast, including projected revenues, backlogs, operating margins, and capital investments. BCA's leadership team reviews the business plan weekly to track the division's performance relative to the plan and to keep the organization focused on execution.

The weekly reviews were invaluable as a performance-monitoring tool at BCA, but they were not particularly effective at bringing new issues to the surface or driving strategic decision making. So in 2001, the unit's leadership team introduced a Strategy Integration Process focused on uncovering and addressing the business's most important strategic issues (such as determining the best go-to-market strategy for the business, driving the evolution of BCA's product strategy, or fueling growth in services). The team assigned to this process holds strategy integration meetings every Monday to track BCA's progress in resolving these long-term issues. Once a specific course of action is agreed upon and approved by BCA's leadership team, the long-range business plan is updated at the next weekly review to reflect the projected change in financial performance.

The time invested in the new decision-making process is more than compensated for by the time saved in the LRBP process, which is now solely focused on strategy execution. The company gets the best of both worlds—disciplined decision making and superior execution. BCA has maintained the value of the LRBP as an execution tool even as it has increased the quality and quantity of important decisions. Managers believe that the new process is at least partially responsible for the sharp turnaround in Boeing's performance since 2001.

They focus on a few key themes

High-performing companies typically focus their strategy discussions on a limited number of important issues or themes, many of which span multiple businesses. Moving away from a business-by-business planning model in this way has proved particularly helpful for large, complex organizations, where strategy discussions can quickly get bogged down as each division manager attempts to cover every aspect of the unit's strategy. Business-unit managers should remain involved in corporate-level strategy planning that affects their units. But a focus on issues rather than business units better aligns strategy development with decision making and investment.

Consider Microsoft. The world's leading software maker is a highly matrixed organization. No strategy can be effectively executed at the company without careful coordination across multiple functions and across two or more of Microsoft's seven business units, or, as executives refer to them, "P&Ls"—Client; Server and Tools; Information Worker; MSN; Microsoft Business Solutions; Mobile and Embedded Devices; and Home and Entertainment. In late 2004, faced with a perceived shortage of good investment ideas, CEO Steve Ballmer asked Robert Uhlaner, Microsoft's corporate vice president of strategy, planning, and analysis, to devise a new strategic planning process for the company. Uhlaner put in place a Growth and Performance Planning Process that starts with agreement by Ballmer's leadership team on a set of strategic themes—major issues like PC market growth, the entertainment market, and security—that cross business-unit boundaries. These themes not only frame the dialogue for Microsoft's annual strategy review, they also guide the units in fleshing out investment alternatives to fuel the company's growth. Dialogues between the P&L leaders and Ballmer's team focus on what the company can do to address each strategic theme, rather than on individual unit strategies. The early results of this new process are promising. "You have to be careful what you wish for," Uhlaner says. "Our new process has surfaced countless new opportunities for growth. We no longer worry about a dearth of investment ideas, but how best to fund them."

The Disconnect Between Planning and Decision Making

How Executives Plan

66% periodically

Percentage of surveyed executives saying their companies conduct strategic planning only at prescribed times

67% unit by unit

Percentage saying planning is done unit by unit

How Executives Decide

100% continuously

Percentage of executives saying strategic decisions are made without regard to the calendar

70% issue by issue

Percentage saying decisions are made issue by issue

No wonder only 11% of executives are highly satisfied that strategic planning is worth the effort.

Like Microsoft, Diageo North America—a division of the international beer, wine, and spirits marketer—has recently changed the way it conducts strategic planning to allocate resources across its diverse portfolio. Diageo historically focused its planning efforts on individual brands. Brand managers were allowed to make the case for additional investment, no matter what the size of the brand or its strategic role in the portfolio. As a result, resource allocation was bedeviled by endless negotiations between the brands and corporate management. This political wrangling made it extremely difficult for Diageo's senior managers to establish a consistent approach to growth, because a lack of transparency prevented them from discerning, from the many requests for additional funding, which brands really deserved more resources and which did not.

Starting in 2001, Diageo overhauled its approach to strategy development. A crucial change was to focus planning on the factors that the company believed would most drive market growth—for example, an increase in the U.S. Hispanic population. By modeling the impact of these factors on the brand portfolio, Diageo has been better able to match its resources with the brands that have the most growth potential so that it can specify the strategies and investments each brand manager should develop, says Jim Moseley, senior vice president of consumer planning and research for Diageo North America. For example, the division now identifies certain brands for growth and earmarks specific resources for investment in these units. This focused approach has enabled the company to shorten the brand planning process and reduce the time spent on negotiations between the brands and division management. It has also given senior management greater confidence in each brand's ability to contribute to Diageo's growth.

They make strategy development continuous
Effective strategy planners spread strategy reviews throughout the year rather than squeeze them into a two- or three-month window. This allows senior executives to focus on one issue at a time until they reach a decision or set of decisions. Moreover, managers can add issues to the agenda as market and competitive conditions change, so there's no need for ad hoc processes. Senior executives can thus rely on a single strategic planning process—or, perhaps more aptly, a single strategic decision-making model—to drive decision making across the company.

Textron, a $10 billion multi-industry company, has implemented a new, continuous strategy-development process built around a prioritized "decision agenda" comprising the company's most important issues and opportunities. Until 2004, Textron had a fairly traditional strategic planning process. Each spring, the company's operating units—businesses as diverse as Bell Helicopter, E-Z-Go golf cars, and Jacobsen turf maintenance equipment—would develop a five-year strategic plan based on standard templates. Unit managers would then review their strategic plans with Textron's management committee (the company's top five executives) during daylong sessions at each unit. Once the strategy reviews were complete, the units incorporated the results, as best they could, into their annual operating plans and capital budgets.

In June 2004, dissatisfied with the quality and pace of the decision making that resulted from the company's strategy reviews, CEO Lewis Campbell asked Stuart Grief, Textron's vice president for strategy and business development, to rethink the company's strategic planning process. After carefully reviewing the company's practices and gathering feedback from its 30 top executives, Grief and his team designed a new Textron Strategy Process.

There were two important changes. First, rather than concentrate all of the operating-unit strategy reviews in the second quarter of each year, the company now spreads strategy dialogues throughout the year—two to three units are reviewed per quarter. Second, rather than organize the management committee dialogues around business-unit plans, Textron now holds continuous reviews that are designed to address each strategic issue on the company's decision agenda. Both changes have enabled Textron's management committee to be much more effectively engaged in business-unit strategy development. The changes have also ensured that there's a forum in which cross-unit issues can be raised and addressed by top management, with input from relevant business-unit managers. The process has significantly increased the number of strategic decisions the company makes each year. As a result, Textron has gone from being an also-ran among its multi-industrial peers to a top-quartile performer over the past 18 months.

John Cullivan, the director of strategy at Cardinal Health, one of the world's leading health-care products and services companies, reports similar benefits from shifting to a continuous planning model. "Continuous decision making is tough to establish because it requires the reallocation of management time at the top levels of the company," he says. "But the process has enabled us to get sharper focus on the short-term performance of our vertical businesses and make faster progress on our longer-term priorities, some of which are horizontal opportunities that cut across businesses and thus are difficult to manage."

To facilitate continuous strategic decision making, Cardinal has made a series of important changes to its traditional planning process. At the corporate level, for example, the company has put in place a rolling six-month agenda for its executive committee dialogues, a practice that allows everyone inside Cardinal to know what issues management is working on and when decisions will be reached. Similar decision agendas are used at the business-unit and functional levels, ensuring that common standards are applied to all important decisions at the company. And to support continuous decision making at Cardinal, the company has trained "black belts" in new analytical tools and processes and deployed them throughout the organization. This provides each of the company's businesses and functions with the resources needed to address strategic priorities that emerge over time.

They structure strategy reviews to produce real decisions

The most common obstacles to decision making at large companies are disagreements among executives over past decisions, current alternatives, and even the facts presented to support strategic plans. Leading companies structure their strategy review sessions to overcome these problems.

At Textron, for example, strategic-issue reviews are organized around "facts, alternatives, and choices." Each issue is addressed in two half-day sessions with the company's management committee, allowing for eight to ten issues to be resolved throughout the year. In the first session, the management committee debates and reaches agreement on the relevant facts—information on the profitability of key markets, the actions of competitors, the purchase behavior of customers, and so on—and a limited set of viable strategy alternatives. The purpose of this first meeting is not to reach agreement on a specific course of action; rather, the meeting ensures that the group has the best possible information and a robust set of alternatives to consider. The second session is focused on evaluating these alternatives from a strategic and financial perspective and selecting the best course of action. By separating the dialogue around facts and alternatives from the debate over choices, Textron's management committee avoids many of the bottlenecks that plague strategic decision making at most companies and reaches many more decisions than it otherwise would.

Like Textron, Cadbury Schweppes has changed the structure of its strategy dialogues to focus top managers more explicitly on decision making. In 2002, after acquiring and integrating gum-maker Adams—a move that significantly expanded Cadbury's product and geographic reach—the company realized it needed to rethink how it was conducting dialogues about strategy between the corporate center and the businesses. The company made two important changes. First, strategy dialogues were redesigned to incorporate a standard set of facts and metrics about consumers, customers, and competitors. This information helped get critical commercial choices in front of top managers, so that the choices were no longer buried in the business units. Second, senior executives' time was reallocated so they could pay more attention to markets that were crucial to realizing Cadbury's ten-year vision and to making important decisions.

Cadbury's top team now spends one full week per year in each of the countries that are most critical to driving the company's performance, so that important decisions can be informed by direct observation as well as through indirect analysis. Strategy dialogues are now based on a much deeper understanding of the markets. Cadbury's strategic reviews no longer merely consist of reviews of and approval of a strategic plan, and they produce many more important decisions.

Done right, strategic planning can have an enormous impact on a company's performance and long-term value. By creating a planning process that enables managers to discover great numbers of hidden strategic issues and make more decisions, companies will open the door to many more opportunities for long-term growth and profitability. By embracing decision-focused planning, companies will almost certainly find that the quantity and quality of their decisions will improve. And—no coincidence—they will discover an improvement in the quality of the dialogue between senior corporate managers and unit managers. Corporate executives will gain a better understanding of the challenges their companies face, and unit managers will benefit fully from the experience and insights of the company's leaders. As Mark Reckitt, a director of group strategy at Cadbury Schweppes, puts it: "Continuous, decision-focused strategic planning has helped our top management team to streamline its agenda and work with business units and functional management to make far better business-strategy and commercial decisions."

Originally published in January 2006. Reprint R0601F

MAHZARIN R. BANAJI is the Richard Clarke Cabot Professor of Social Ethics at Harvard University.

MAX H. BAZERMAN is the Jesse Isidor Straus Professor of Business Administration at Harvard Business School.

MARCIA BLENKO is a Bain partner in Boston and leads the firm's global organization practice.

ANDREW CAMPBELL is a director of Ashridge Strategic Management Centre in London.

RAM CHARAN is a business author and adviser. He was on the faculties of Harvard Business School and Northwestern's Kellogg School.

DOLLY CHUGH is an assistant professor of management and organizations at New York University's Stern School of Business.

THOMAS H. DAVENPORT is the President's Distinguished Professor of Information Technology and Management at Babson College.

ROBIN L. DILLON is an associate professor at Georgetown's McDonough School of Business.

SYDNEY FINKELSTEIN is the Steven Roth Professor of Management at the Tuck School of Business at Dartmouth College.

DAVID A. GARVIN is the C. Roland Christensen Professor of Business Administration at Harvard Business School.

JOHN S. HAMMOND is a consultant on decision making and a former professor at Harvard Business School.

DANIEL KAHNEMAN is a senior scholar at the Woodrow Wilson School of Public and International Affairs at Princeton University and a partner at the consultancy The Greatest Good. He was awarded the

Nobel Prize in Economic Sciences in 2002 for his work (with Amos Tversky) on cognitive biases.

RALPH L. KEENEY is a professor emeritus at Duke University's Fuqua School of Business.

DAN LOVALLO is a professor of business strategy at the University of Sydney and a senior adviser to McKinsey & Company.

PETER M. MADSEN is an assistant professor at Brigham Young University's Marriott School of Management.

MICHAEL C. MANKINS is a partner at Bain & Company. He is based in San Francisco and heads the firm's North America organization practice.

HOWARD RAIFFA is the Frank Plumpton Ramsey Professor of Managerial Economics (Emeritus) at Harvard Business School.

MICHAEL A. ROBERTO is the Trustee Professor of Management at Bryant University.

PAUL ROGERS leads Bain & Company's London office.

OLIVIER SIBONY is a director in the Paris office of McKinsey & Company.

RICHARD STEELE is a partner at The Bridgespan Group and heads the firm's New York office.

CATHERINE H. TINSLEY is a professor of management and head of the management group at Georgetown's McDonough School of Business.

JO WHITEHEAD is a director of Ashridge Strategic Management Centre in London.

Index

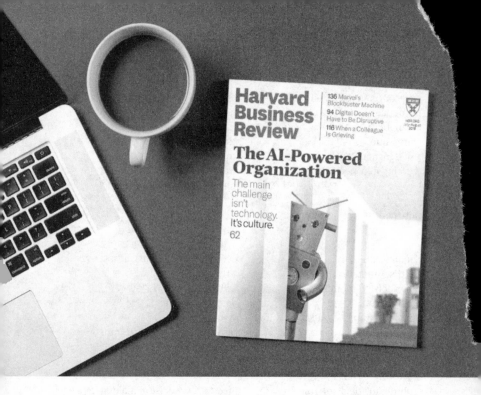

Engage with HBR content the way you want, on any device.

With HBR's new subscription plans, you can access world-renowned **case studies** from Harvard Business School and receive **four free eBooks**. Download and customize prebuilt **slide decks and graphics** from our **Visual Library**. With HBR's archive, top 50 best-selling articles, and five new articles every day, HBR is more than just a magazine.

Subscribe Today
hbr.org/success